FAITH WALK

DISCIPLE'S MANUAL
FAITH WALK

Discipleship for the 21st Century

EDITED BY MICHAEL L. BAKER

Credits:
Cover Design: Wayne Slocumb
Inside Layout: Mark Shuler
Copy Editor: Esther Metaxas

Library of Congress Catalog Card Number: 0-87148-345-9
ISBN: 98-068789

Copyright © 1999 by Pathway Press
Cleveland, Tennessee 37311
All Rights Reserved
Printed in the United States of America

CONTENTS

FOREWORD

The church is made up of people—individuals who have responded to the call of Christ to follow Him. In Matthew 28:18-20, Christ's command to His church was to produce a fruit-bearing believer called a *disciple*.

Recognizing that God calls believers into a variety of vocations and ministries, the church must accept its responsibility to nurture believers to identify and develop their unique spiritual gifts God has given for the expansion of His kingdom. The church must lead believers to live an abundant life in the Spirit.

Discipleship is personal spiritual growth and maturity that leads to a deepening relationship with God. It includes learning the Bible's teachings and living out those teachings in daily life. *FAITH WALK* will help lead believers to grow in their walk with Christ. This study will assist in orienting believers to the beliefs and practices of New Testament Christianity.

The imperative command of Christ is to "go and make disciples of all nations" (Matthew 28:19). It is a call—a call to serve. The primary calling is to share the "good news" leading others to follow Him. It is the formula for evangelizing the world. Trained and committed disciples are the work force of God and discipleship is the heart of the church.

When you have completed *FAITH WALK* your life will be enriched by an understanding of the Declaration of Faith and its scriptural undergirding. You will better share the reason for the hope that is within you.

Paul L. Walker, Ph.D.

INTRODUCTION

PURPOSE

FAITH WALK is a twelve-lesson interactive study for believers. It is designed for use with small groups or personal individual study. The purpose of the course is to help Christians become familiar with Biblical doctrine. This book is based on the Church of God Declaration of Faith, which is similar to the faith statements of most Pentecostal and Charismatic churches.

SMALL GROUPS

The study groups can vary in size. The suggested group size is no more than fifteen. In addition, the study can be completed individually. However, small study groups allow for greater interaction between students and instructor.

Within the life of a church, believers have an interest in understanding basic Biblical doctrine. An important key to spiritual growth and development is the implementation of a perpetual discipleship program and ministry. *FAITH WALK* is designed for twelve sessions with the possibility of multiple discipleship-training groups operating simultaneously based upon need. There may be an immediate need to begin a discipleship-training group and within a few weeks there are more persons who wish to begin their discipleship study. At any one point in time, there could be many different small groups meeting simultaneously in discipleship ministry.

STUDY FORMAT

FAITH WALK is an interactive study written in simple and understandable language. It includes essential elements and sections common to each lesson. Included in the lesson format are the following elements:

INTRODUCTION. An *introduction* to the discipleship topic is presented along with other topic headings throughout the study lesson.

DECLARATION OF FAITH. The Declaration of Faith statement is qouted from the Church of God official document. Supporting scripture references have been added.

SCRIPTURAL FOCUS. The *scriptural focus* provides scriptural references directly related to the topic discussion. All scripture quotations are *NKJV* (New King James Version) throughout unless otherwise noted.

APPLYING THE TRUTH—My Daily Walk with Christ. These sections call for specific action steps or interactive response to the topic discussion. Many of the activities are designed to lead the student to interaction with God through meditation, prayer, commitment and Bible study.

LESSON REVIEW. The *lesson review* succinctly summaries the topic of the lesson and brings to a conclusion the discussion.

DISCIPLESHIP INSIGHTS. These concise statements share the heart of the lesson. When each lesson is completed, these insights help the student to remember and understand key issues that were presented and discussed.

NOTES and *RESOURCES*. Each lesson provides space for personal notes, as well as a listing of resource materials for further study.

WHERE AND WHEN

The discipleship program can utilize multiple delivery systems to accommodate the differences in learning style and lifestyles of believers. For example, sessions could be scheduled during regular church services, Sunday school, weekday mornings or evenings, before or after work or in a designated home. Where and when sessions are scheduled can be determined by the members to meet their specific needs. It should be noted that flexibility in scheduling will help to determine a "right" time and place. Regardless of what is chosen, there may be adjustments.

PARTICIPATION

Study materials in *FAITH WALK* are self-paced and interactive. Students are encouraged to study and pray prior to each scheduled meeting of the group. Attendance is important for both the student and group. Each discipleship student should make a firm commitment of participation.

RESOURCES NEEDED

Each member of the group will need a copy of the Disciple's Manual and a Bible. Students may desire to use other personal materials for notes and further study. The instructor's guide is provided as a separate volume.

Michael L. Baker, Editor

Verbal Inspiration of the Bible

LESSON 1

Donald M. Walker

INTRODUCTION

The Way to God

In the world today there are millions of people who are searching for a true source and guide of authority. The only real authority that we have is the Word of God. It reveals human nature, human suffering and world problems. But beyond anything else that the Bible does, it reveals very clearly the way to God.

The Lord Jesus Christ is the central message of the Bible. Jesus said, "I am the way, the truth, and the life" (John 14:6). The Bible gives us the account of salvation and redemption through Christ—the beautiful story of life, peace and eternity.

Relevant

The Bible is relevant to our generation. It speaks to the needs of this society and culture. The Scriptures reveal to us the answers to vital and ultimate questions such as these: Where did I come from? Why am I here? Where am I going? What is the purpose of my existence?

There is a need in the church today to study the Scriptures and recognize the Bible as the basis of authority.

The Scriptures

The Scriptures in both the Old and New Testaments reveal God's incarnate Son—the Lord Jesus Christ. Jesus Christ said in Matthew 4:4, "Man shall not live by bread alone, but by every word that proceeds from the mouth of God." John 5:39 says, "Search the Scriptures . . . they . . . testify of Me." There cannot be growth or maturity in the life of a Christian separated from the knowledge and understanding of the Word of God. The Word of God must be priority in the believer's daily living.

The Bible is the standard of living relating to a personal faith, morals, practical living, holiness, and effectiveness in service and performance.

One must give attention to the reading of the Word of God with intention. The intention will necessitate attention. One reason there is far too little Bible reading today is that there is so little intention given to God's Word.

Intention

We are all busy but must take time to read the Word of God. If we are going to know the Bible, we must give time to it. We must arrange our lives so that time is made for reading of God's Word. Unless we do, we shall never come into any worthy knowledge of the truth. It is the truth of God's Word that sets us free: "And you shall know the truth, and the truth shall make you free" (John 8:32).

Time

The Bible reveals the will of God. Each book of the Bible has a direct message and application. We must know what that message is and conform to it. This must be our purpose. We must understand primarily how the Scripture became the very Word of God.

Message

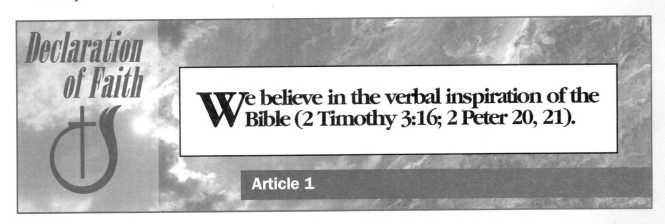

Declaration of Faith

We believe in the verbal inspiration of the Bible (2 Timothy 3:16; 2 Peter 20, 21).

Article 1

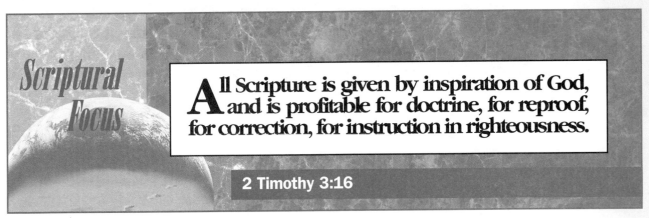

Scriptural Focus

All Scripture is given by inspiration of God, and is profitable for doctrine, for reproof, for correction, for instruction in righteousness.

2 Timothy 3:16

The Church of God rejects:

Alternate Views

- The agnostic view, which objects to the divine origin of the Bible and confesses only its sublimity as literature.

- The "liberal religionist" view, which compromises to assert that the Bible only *contains* the Word of God.

- The concept that those who wrote the Scriptures did it through their supersensitivity or aesthetic response to spiritual matters.

◆ The "Concept Theory," which holds that God revealed His truth to holy men and left to their disposition the precise words to be used.

◆ The view that the writers of the Scriptures were mere machines with God dictating each word. "Holy men of God spoke as they were moved by the Holy Spirit" (2 Peter 1:21). The variety of style through the Scriptures emphasizes the fact of individual expression.

THE HOLY SCRIPTURES

Revelation

The Bible is God's written revelation of His will to men. The central theme of the Bible is salvation through Jesus Christ. The Bible contains 66 books, written by 40 authors, covering a period of more that 1,600 years. The Bible consists of the Old Testament and the New Testament. The Old Testament was written mostly in Hebrew, and about 200 years before the Christian era the entire Old Testament was translated into Greek. The New Testament was written in the Greek language.

Testament

The word *testament* means "covenant" or "agreement." The Old Testament is the covenant that God made with man about His salvation before Christ came. The New Testament is the agreement God made with man about his salvation after Christ came.

The title "Holy Bible" is rightly derived from the fact that the holy God is its author.

The writers of the Scriptures were so moved by God's Holy Spirit that God's Word can affirm that they "spoke from God." Jesus stated that what the Scriptures said can be described as what God said (Matthew 19:4, 5; see also Romans 9:17). The Bible is not merely revelational in encounter nor is it merely a witness to revelation. It is God's objective revelation to man.

No errors

The Old and New Testaments affirm thousands of times that the Bible is the Word of God. To those who may argue that there may be error in God's Word, we can only respond that since the very words of Scripture originated with God (1 Corinthians 2:13) and God cannot err (Hebrews 6:18; Titus 1:2), the Scripture cannot err.

The Scripture thus receives authority from God himself and not from the church or any other human source (1 Thessalonians 2:13).

The Old Testament is the covenant of law; the New Testament is the covenant of grace, which came through Jesus Christ.

Verbal Inspiration

In this lesson we will look at the verbal inspiration of the Bible. The first article of Church of God Declaration of Faith is that we believe in the verbal inspiration of the Bible.

Doctrine

We believe that all Scripture is of God and therefore true (John 17:17). There is no authoritative source, other than the Scriptures themselves, from which doctrine can be established.

According to our Lord Jesus Christ, the serious Biblical errors of men are due to the fact that they know neither the Scriptures nor the power of God (Mark 12:24).

A Christian must follow Christ in his view of Scripture. Jesus said that if people would believe in the Scripture, they would also believe Him (John 5:39-47).

TRUE SOURCE OF CHRISTIAN DOCTRINE

Theology

The Bible is recognized as the true source of Christian theology. It is necessary to understand that the authority of the Holy Scriptures is the true record of the historical development and the finished result of divine revelation.

The Bible is not merely a book, it is *the* Book—the book that from the importance of its subjects, the wideness of its ranges, and the majority of its authors stands as high above all other books as the heaven is high above the earth. The Bible is our basic instruction while on earth—consequently, the true source of Christian doctrine.

HOW THEN DID WE RECEIVE THE BIBLE?

Three Ways

The Scriptures were shaped in three different ways: (1) Revelation, which means man hears that which God wants written; (2) Inspiration, which means man writes that which God wants written; and (3) Illumination, which means man receives the light of that which God has written.

REVELATION

Revelation is that act of God by which He directly communicates truth not known before to the human mind.

Revelation discovers new truth while inspiration superintends the communication of that truth.

By revelation we mean a direct communication from God to man of such knowledge as was beyond his usual abilities to attain.

Verbal Inspiration

The term *verbally* indicates that all of the words of the Bible, not merely its concepts, are inspired.

The word *verbal* means "of or pertaining to words; consisting in or having to do with words only, dealing with words rather than the ideas to be conveyed."

The term *inspired* does not refer to heightened forms of human insight or to an intensified appreciation for divine truth; rather, it means that scriptures are to be considered as the very "breath" of God. Just as spoken words are the product of human breath, so the written Scriptures are the product of the divine breath—that work of God in inspiring the human authors so that what they recorded was in reality His Word.

God-breathed

The writers were not used as machines but were "moved" (borne along) by the Holy Spirit (2 Peter 1:21) resulting that the Scriptures are "God-breathed" (2 Timothy 3:16, *NIV*).

Inspiration is the strong, conscious "inbreathing" of God into men, qualifying them to give utterance to truth. It is God speaking through man.

The Bible is, in deed and in truth, the very Word of God, and the books of the Bible are of divine origin and authority.

INSPIRATION

Literary Miracle

This leads even the most simple to conclude that the Bible is nothing short of a divine miracle. The Bible is a literary miracle. A long-range miracle!

How could God, over all this span of years, bring this miracle to pass? The answer is divine inspiration! "All Scripture is given by inspiration of God" (2 Timothy 3:16).

The word *inspired* means literally "God-breathed." It is composed of two Greek words—*theos* (God) and *pneo* (to breathe). The term "given by inspiration," signifies that the writings of the Scriptures are the result of a certain influence exerted by God upon authors. Inspiration is the strong, conscious inbreathing of God into men, qualifying them to give utterance to truth. It is God speaking through men. The Scriptures, therefore, are just as much the Word of God as though God spoke every single word with His own lips.

"For the prophecy came not in old time by the will of man: but Holy men of God spoke as they were moved by the Holy Ghost" (2 Peter 2:21).

The passive participle translated "when moved" distinctly teaches that the Scriptures were not written by mere men, or at their suggestion, but by men moved upon, prompted, driven, by the prompting of the Holy Ghost.

Inspiration has been defined as "the inexplicable power which the divine spirit put forth of old on the authors of the Holy Scripture, to their guidance, even in the employment of the words they used, and to preserve them alike from all error and from all omission." *Inspire* means "God breathed." God did not just breath into them, but he actually breathed *the word* into them, so every word is created by God.

Here we are in deep mystery! We cannot understand divine inspiration, but we must believe it. God wrote the Book, but God used man. These are the two sides of the coin. No explanation or illustration exists that can satisfy us.

Yet the best illustration is that of the Lord Jesus as He became at once God in human flesh. We know that He did not cease to be God. He became what he was not—yet he never ceased to be what he was. Christ was at once very God and very man. Here we have the mystery and miracle of the two natures in one man. It is wrong to try to explain away Christ's divine nature in order to understand His human nature. It is wrong to try to explain away Christ's human nature in order to understand His divine nature. We must accept both of these truths as the Word of God presents them. But to understand them is another thing. So just as Jesus is both at once divine and human, so this book is divine and human. Our mistake is to try to explain the unexplainable and to fathom the unfathomable. We don't need to worry about how the Word got here, but we are to believe that it is here and that we must obey it.

ILLUMINATION

Without inspiration no portion of the Scripture would have been written. Without illumination no sinner would have ever been saved. Illumination is that method used by the Holy Spirit to shed divine light upon all who seek as they look into the Word of God. Illumination is from the written Word to the human heart (Matthew 16:16, 17).

Illumination

Illumination is not automatic. God never promised to reveal Biblical truths to any believer who will not search the Scriptures (Matthew 4:4; 2 Timothy 2:15). Sinful people cannot experience illumination in this sense, for they are blinded to the truth of God (1 Corinthians 2:14).

Searching

Illumination describes the enlightening experience of conversion (Hebrews 6:4), the understanding of Christian truth (Ephesians 1:18; 3:9) and the searching character of further judgment (1 Corinthians 4:5).

Illumination is the work of the Holy Spirit making clear the truth of the written revelation.

CONCLUSION

The Church of God believes that inspiration from a theological view is the operation of the Holy Spirit upon those who wrote the Bible in such perfect measure that what they wrote became the expression of God's will to man; the whole Bible is completely and equally inspired; the Bible is the written Word of God and the very Word of God; and that the entire Bible is God-breathed. We understand *inspiration* to mean "God-breathed" or the "breathing of God," that is, the supernatural inbreathing of God upon the physical senses of holy men. This inbreathing was so absolute that that which was written was the supreme truth of God.

Completely Inspired

Without impairing the intelligence, individuality, literary style or personal feelings of the human authors, God supernaturally directed the writing of Scripture so that they recorded in perfect accuracy His comprehensive and infallible revelation to man. If God himself had done the writing, the written Word would be no more accurate and authoritative than it is.

Supernatural Direction

By means of divine inspiration the writers of Scripture spoke with authority concerning the unknown past, wrote by divine guidance the historical portions, revealed the law, penned the devotional literature of the Bible, recorded the contemporary prophetic message, and prophesied the future.

Life's Priority

The priority in the life of every believer is the fact that we must read the Word of God, study the Word of God and memorize the Word of God.

The Word of God—the Bible—is the inspired Word of God and is our only source of wisdom, knowledge and understanding of the truth that is of ultimate and eternal significance.

Paul told Timothy to "give attention to reading [God's Word], to exhortation, to doctrine" (1 Timothy 4:13).

We must reaffirm our belief in the trustworthiness of the Holy Scriptures and pledge ourselves to uphold, by our lifestyle and testimony, that we believe in the verbal inspiration of the Bible.

Applying the Truth

MY DAILY WALK WITH GOD

List the ways you will discipline yourself to read and study the Word of God. _____

_____

_____

List the reasons the Word of God is so significant in your life, marriage, family, work, and so forth. _____

_____

_____

_____

Why is it important to believe the Bible is the inspired Word of God?

_____

_____

_____

List the strategy and system you will use to consistently study the Word of God. _____

_____

Read carefully 2 Timothy 3:16, 17. Prayerfully study and write in your own words what this passage of Scripture means to you.

_____

_____

_____

_____

Consider selecting some friends in your local church or another local church to study and discuss the Bible—how it came to be and what it means to you personally.

Consider asking your pastor to do a study from Charles Conn's book *The Bible—Book of Books*. You will find this study to be personally informative and inspiring.

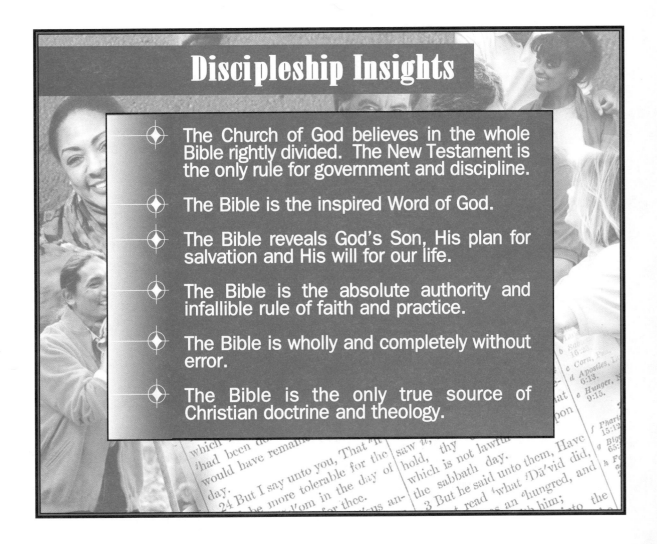

Discipleship Insights

- The Church of God believes in the whole Bible rightly divided. The New Testament is the only rule for government and discipline.

- The Bible is the inspired Word of God.

- The Bible reveals God's Son, His plan for salvation and His will for our life.

- The Bible is the absolute authority and infallible rule of faith and practice.

- The Bible is wholly and completely without error.

- The Bible is the only true source of Christian doctrine and theology.

BIBLE STATISTICS:

The Bible contains:	OLD TESTAMENT	NEW TESTAMENT
66 Books	39 Books	27 Books
	17 Historical	4 Gospels
	5 Poetical	1 Historical
	17 Prophetic	21 Epistles
		1 Prophetic
1,189 Chapters	929 Chapters	260 Chapters

Longest Chapter	Psalm 119
Shortest Chapter	Psalm 117 (also the middle chapter of the Bible)
Longest Verse	Esther 8:9
Shortest Verse	John 11:35

Written over a period of 1,600 years

40 Different Writers

ENGLISH TRANSLATIONS

- Caedmon (A.D. 667)
- Bede (672-735)
- Alfred the Great (849-901)—translated short parts of the Bible into Anglo-Saxon
- Wycliffe's Bible (A.D. 1382)—first English Bible
- Tyndale's Bible (1525)—translated from the original Greek and Hebrew; more accurate than Wycliffe's
- Coverdale's Bible (1525)—from Dutch and Latin sources
- Roger's Bible (1560)
- "The Great Bible" (1539)—a compilation from Tyndale, Rogers and Coverdale
- Geneva Bible (1560)
- King James Version (1611)—a revision of versions based on Tyndale's. For nearly 400 years it has been the household Bible of the English-speaking world.
- Anglo-American Revision (1881-1885)
- American Edition (1901)
- Revised Standard Version (1946)
- New International Version (1973)
- New King James Version (1979)
- New Living Translation (1996)
- Numerous other translations

Resources

Mears, Henrietta C. *What the Bible Is All About*. Minneapolis: Billy Graham Evangelistic Association.

Pache, René. *The Inspiration and Authority of Scripture*. Chicago: Moody Press, 1980.

Conn, Charles W. *The Bible—Book of Books*. Cleveland, TN: Pathway Press, 1961.

Willmington, H.L. *Willmington's Guide to the Bible*. Wheaton, IL: Tyndale House Publishers, 1984.

NOTES:_____

_____

_____

_____

_____

_____

_____

_____

_____

_____

_____

_____

_____

_____

_____

_____

_____

_____

_____

_____

TRINITY

One God Eternally Existing in Three Persons

LESSON 2

Grant McClung

INTRODUCTION

Trinity

This lesson will focus on one of the most encouraging facts of the Bible: that our everlasting and eternal God relates to us as one God who eternally exists in three persons—Father, Son, and Holy Spirit. We will see how both the Old and New Testaments reveal the truth of God as a trinity—as a triune God. We will see how each of the three persons is God in each of their distinct personalities and roles, and yet how they are one in essence, unity and purpose. The overall goal of our study is to lead us into the Scriptures for instruction on who our God is and how we are to worship and serve Him.

Our belief in this Biblical teaching is stated in the second article of the Church of God Declaration of Faith.

Declaration of Faith

We believe in one God eternally existing in three persons; namely, the Father, Son, and Holy Ghost (Matthew 3:16, 17; 28:19; 2 Corinthians 13:14).

Article 2

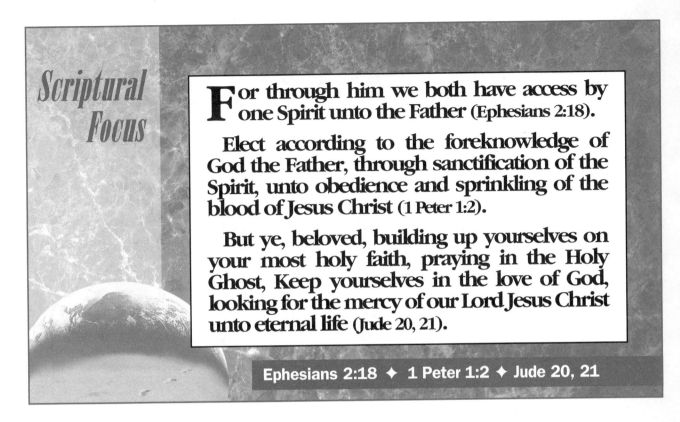

For through him we both have access by one Spirit unto the Father (Ephesians 2:18).

Elect according to the foreknowledge of God the Father, through sanctification of the Spirit, unto obedience and sprinkling of the blood of Jesus Christ (1 Peter 1:2).

But ye, beloved, building up yourselves on your most holy faith, praying in the Holy Ghost, Keep yourselves in the love of God, looking for the mercy of our Lord Jesus Christ unto eternal life (Jude 20, 21).

Ephesians 2:18 ✦ 1 Peter 1:2 ✦ Jude 20, 21

This faith declaration agrees with a statement of belief from the early years of the Christian movement. It was called the Athanasian Creed and it stated, "So the Father is God; the Son is God; and the Holy Ghost is God. And yet there are not three gods, but one God."

GOD IS THE MODEL FOR THE PENTECOSTAL EXPERIENCE

One of our fellow Pentecostals who helps us understand the triune God is Dr. French L. Arrington, who writes about "The Holy Trinity" in his book *Christian Doctrine: A Pentecostal Perspective*, Volume One. We will use Dr. Arrington's study as an outline to lead us into a discussion of some Biblical passages about the triune God. Here is what Dr. Arrington says about the relationship of each personality of the triune Godhead to one another and how this is an example for those of us who follow in the "Pentecostal faith walk":

Triune God

The doctrine of the Trinity stresses the perfect fellowship and relationship within the triune God. The three persons of the Godhead enjoy the closest ties of love and common purpose. The personal relationship within the Trinity has special significance for the Pentecostal experience. The Holy Spirit, for example, has endued the Pentecostal believer with power for service consistent with the commissioning of Jesus Christ, God's Son (see Luke 3:21, 22; 4:1, 18, 19). As Jesus Christ was called by God the Father and anointed with the power of the Holy Spirit, Pentecostal believers have been called of God and endued with the

Three Persons —One God

power of the Holy Spirit. As the anointing of Jesus was an example of the perfect relationship of the Father, the Son, and the Holy Spirit, so is the Pentecostal's experience. This fact became clear in the outpouring of the Holy Spirit as told in Acts 2. The disciples' experience of the Holy Spirit on that occasion flowed from the victorious Christ; but the Holy Spirit, whom He gave, had been promised by the Father (Acts 2:33). At the very heart of the Pentecostal experience is the work of the triune God. He is always present in all of His works (pp. 127-128).

Applying the Truth
MY DAILY WALK WITH GOD

As a statement of belief and worship, repeat aloud (either individually or together as a group) Article 2 of the Declaration of Faith: "We [I] believe in one God eternally existing in three persons; namely, the Father, Son, and Holy Ghost."

Praise God that He has eternally existed as one God in three persons.

Worship each member of the triune Godhead by name (Father, Son, and Holy Spirit). Thank each One for how they relate individually to one another in perfect fellowship and unity. Praise God for how the Father, the Son, and the Holy Spirit relate to you individually and to your fellow faith walkers collectively.

Use group and individual prayers. A hymn (such as "Holy, Holy, Holy") or a chorus can be used for worship. Here's a commonly used worship chorus:

Heavenly Father, I appreciate You.
Heavenly Father, I appreciate You.
I love You, adore You, I bow down before You.
Heavenly Father, I appreciate You.

Son of God, what a wonder You are.
Son of God, what a wonder You are.
You've cleansed my soul from sin, put the Holy Ghost within.
Son of God, what a wonder You are.

Holy Spirit, You're a comfort to me.
Holy Spirit, You're a comfort to me.
You lead me, You guide me, You live right inside me.
Holy Spirit, You're a comfort to me.

Arranged by Don Marsh. ©Copyright 1975 by John T. Benson Pub. Co. *Lift Him Up.* Compiled by Don Marsh. Nashville, TN: Benson Co., 1977.

As a prayer request, ask that the unity and perfect fellowship of the Trinity will be realized in our group fellowship in our church and families.

Pray also that the triune God will reveal Himself and come close to you and each one as you continue in this study.

Dr. Arrington has said that the personal experience of Jesus and of the early disciples on the Day of Pentecost (Acts 2) are an example of how we can experience the triune God as Pentecostal believers. Read the scriptures listed below aloud.

When all the people were being baptized, Jesus was baptized too. And as he was praying, heaven was opened and the Holy Spirit descended on him in bodily form like a dove. And a voice came from heaven: "You are my Son, whom I love; with you I am well pleased" (Luke 3:21, 22, *NIV*).

Jesus, being filled with the Holy Spirit, returned from the Jordan and was led by the Spirit . . . (Luke 4:1).

The Spirit of the Lord is on me, because he has anointed me to preach good news to the poor. He has sent me to proclaim freedom for the prisoners and recovery of sight for the blind, to release the oppressed, to proclaim the year of the Lord's favor (Luke 4:18, 19, *NIV*).

How do you see the role and ministry of each of the three personalities of the Trinity in these scriptures? _____

_____

_____

_____

_____

_____

What are the lessons for you as a Pentecostal? _____

_____

_____

_____

_____

Do you have the same Pentecostal experience as Jesus? _____

_____

_____

Look at the description of the Day of Pentecost (Acts 2) and see especially how each of the members of the triune Godhead are honored in the following words from Peter's message:

God has raised this Jesus to life, and we are all witnesses of the fact. Exalted to the right hand of God, he has received from the Father the promised Holy Spirit and has poured out what you now see and hear (Acts 2:32, 33, *NIV*).

THE TRIUNE GOD IN THE OLD TESTAMENT

Plurality

The Bible reveals various names for God. One of them in the Old Testament is *Elohim*: "In the beginning God [Elohim] created . . ." (Genesis 1:1). *Elohim* is plural, meaning more than one person in the Godhead. Consider how the following statement refers to more than one person: "Let Us make man in Our image, according to Our likeness . . ." (Genesis 1:26).

"Us"

Consider how the prophet Isaiah referred to more than one person in God when he said, "And now the Lord God and His Spirit have sent Me" (48:16). Isaiah had a personal encounter with God in the Temple. In his spiritual vision, he heard the angels crying, "Holy, holy, holy is the Lord of hosts" (6:3). Some think that each of the three expressions of "Holy" were meant for each member of the Godhead— Father, Son, and Holy Spirit. Then Isaiah was commissioned by a question from the "one God eternally existing in three persons":

"Whom shall I send, and who will go for Us?" (v. 8).

Here is the revelation of "one God eternally existing in three persons":

"Whom shall I send?" (one God)

"Who will go for us?" (three persons)

Applying the Truth
MY DAILY WALK WITH GOD

If you are studying *Faith Walk* in a group, take time now to do the following:

Read aloud the following verses of Isaiah 6:1-8 in unison:

In the year that King Uzziah died, I saw the Lord seated on a throne, high and exalted, and the train of his robe filled the temple. Above him were seraphs, each with six wings: With two wings they covered their faces, with two they covered their feet, and with two they were flying. And they were calling to one another: "Holy, holy, holy is the Lord Almighty; the whole earth is full of his glory." At the sound of their voices the doorposts and thresholds shook and the temple was filled with smoke. "Woe to me!" I cried. "I am ruined! For I am a man of unclean lips, and I live among a people of unclean lips, and my eyes have seen the King, the Lord Almighty." Then one of the seraphs flew to me with a live coal in his hand, which he had taken with tongs from the altar. With it he touched my mouth and said, "See, this has touched your lips; your guilt is taken away and your sin atoned for." Then I heard the voice of the Lord saying, "Whom shall I send? And who will go for us?" And I said, "Here am I. Send me!" (*NIV*).

Stop to worship the triune God who is so powerfully revealed to Isaiah.

Then, look together at the outstanding hymn by Reginald Heber and J.B. Dykes, which is sung in all the major languages of the world: "Holy, Holy, Holy."

Three separate readers should each read a verse slowly and reverently as a prayer. The group should then sing all three verses as a worship experience with the triune God. After singing, allow various members to individually offer up personal prayers of praise to the "one God eternally existing in three persons."

Holy, holy, holy, Lord God Almighty!
Early in the morning our song shall rise to Thee;
Holy, holy, holy, merciful and mighty!
God in three persons, blessed Trinity!

Holy, holy, holy! All the saints adore Thee,
Casting down their golden crowns around the glassy sea;
Cherubim and seraphim falling down before Thee,
Who wert, and art, and evermore shalt be.

Holy, holy, holy, Lord God Almighty!
All Thy works shall praise Thy name, in earth, and sky, and sea;
Holy, holy, holy, merciful and mighty!
God in three persons, blessed Trinity!

THE TRIUNE GOD IN THE NEW TESTAMENT

As we have already seen in the baptism of Jesus, the triune Godhead of Father, Son, and Holy Spirit is revealed. The Father speaks His approval and love to the Son, and the Holy Spirit descends upon Jesus like a dove (see Matthew 3:16, 17; Luke 3:21, 22).

New Testament Proofs

Read aloud the following verse and look for specific references to the Father, Son, and Holy Spirit. Be ready to answer the questions which follow this Bible reference. Go therefore and make disciples of all the nations, baptizing them in the name of the Father and of the Son and of the Holy Spirit (Matthew 28:19).

Applying the Truth
MY DAILY WALK WITH GOD

How are we to baptize the disciples from all nations? _____

_____

"[May] the grace of the Lord Jesus Christ, and the love of God, and the communion of the Holy Spirit be with you all" (2 Corinthians 13:14).

What is the special gift individually from each member of the tri-

une Godhead? _____

_____

_____

"For through Him [Jesus] we both have access by one Spirit to the Father" (Ephesians 2:18).

According to Ephesians 2:18, how is each member of the Godhead

involved in our salvation? _____

_____

_____

"Elect according to the foreknowledge of God the Father, in sanctification of the Spirit, for obedience . . . of Jesus Christ" (1 Peter 1:2).

Did God the Father know about us and choose us? _____

_____

Have we been sanctified by God the Holy Spirit? _____

_____

Are we to obey Jesus, God the Son? _____

_____

"But you, beloved, building yourselves up on your most holy faith, praying in the Holy Spirit, keep yourselves in the love of God, looking for the mercy of our Lord Jesus Christ unto eternal life" (Jude 20, 21).

Fill in the blanks from Jude 20, 21:

We are to pray in the _____ _____.

We are to keep ourselves in the love of _____.

We are to look for the mercy of our Lord _____ _____.

Look at the command words (verbs) of that verse. How does the triune God help us build up, pray, keep, look?_____

_____

_____

_____

How did each member of the Trinity help Stephen as he was being killed for his faith? _____

_____

_____

_____

How does the triune God minister to persecuted Christians in our world today? _____

_____

_____

_____

"There are different kinds of gifts, but the same Spirit. There are different kinds of service, but the same Lord. There are different kinds of working, but the same God works all of them in all men" (1 Corinthians 12:4-6, *NIV*).

How do you see each of the members of the Trinity revealed?

_____

_____

_____

How many times do you see the word *same*? _____

Does this mean that the "one God eternally existing in three persons" works together in harmony and unity? _____

_____

_____

According to the phrase "in all men" (all believers), is every believer given an opportunity to receive the gifts of the Holy Spirit to serve God? _____

_____

_____

Here is the answer from Dr. Arrington:

> The reality of the Holy Trinity is evident in the manifestation of spiritual gifts. There are varieties of ministries, but they proceed from the same Spirit. There are varieties of ministries, but it is the same Lord (Christ) to whom ultimately all service is rendered. There are many operations of the gifts, but the same God (Father) works in every believer (1 Corinthians 12:4-6) (p. 132).

Stop and talk about how the work of the Trinity in the operation of spiritual gifts can be the answer for the mobilization of all God's people (ministers/clergy and laity, men and women, adults and youth/children, all races and nationalities) for the evangelization of the world.

Take time to pray together, or one at a time, for this to happen in our churches worldwide.

THREE DISTINCT PERSONS OF THE GODHEAD

Distinct Persons

Now it is time to see how the Bible reveals each of the members of the Trinity as fully God. Each of the persons of the triune Godhead coexists equally and with full divinity. Here, we should repeat the basic Declaration of Faith about the triune God: "We believe in one God eternally existing in three persons; namely, the Father, Son, and Holy Ghost." Even though we believe that each member is fully God, we do not believe in three gods. We should repeat the Athanasian Creed from the early church: "So the Father is God; the Son is God; and the Holy Ghost is God. And yet there are not three gods, but one God."

A. GOD THE FATHER IS GOD

"Praise be to the God and Father of our Lord Jesus Christ. . ." (Ephesians 1:3, *NIV*). "I keep asking that the God of our Lord Jesus Christ, the glorious Father, may give you the Spirit of wisdom and revelation, so that you may know him better" (1:17, *NIV*). "For this reason I kneel before the Father, from whom his whole family in heaven and on earth derives its name. I pray that out of his glorious riches he may strengthen you with power through his Spirit in your inner being, so that Christ may dwell in your hearts through faith" (3:14-17, *NIV*).

◆ Look in these above three references from Ephesians. Circle the references to each member of the Trinity: Father, Son, and Holy Spirit.

◆ True/False (circle the correct answer)

According to these passages from Ephesians:

True or False __God the Father is to receive praise.

True or False __God the Father is described as glorious.

True or False __God the Father is the One who gives the Spirit of wisdom.

True or False __God the Father wants us to know Him better.

True or False __We are to kneel before God the Father in worship.

True or False __The whole family of God in heaven and on earth derives its name from God the Father.

B. GOD THE SON IS GOD

In the language of Scripture, God the Father and Jesus, God the Son, are "placed side by side so that it becomes clear they are coequal" (Arrington, p. 134). For example:

Father and Son—Coequal

"Grace to you and peace from God our Father and from the Lord Jesus Christ" (Romans 1:7; see also Galatians 1:3).

According to Arrington, Jesus did what only God can do. He spoke with divine authority. He forgave sins. Stop now to consider Matthew 9:1-8:

> Jesus stepped into a boat, crossed over and came to His own town. Some men brought to him a paralytic, lying on a mat. When Jesus saw their faith, he said to the paralytic, "Take heart, son; your sins are forgiven." At this, some of the teachers of the law said to themselves, "This fellow is blaspheming!" Knowing their thoughts, Jesus said, "Why do you entertain evil thoughts in your hearts? Which is easier: to say, 'Your sins are forgiven,' or to say, 'Get up and walk'? But so that you may know that the Son of Man has authority on earth to forgive sins. . . ." Then he said to the paralytic, "Get up, take your mat and go home." And the man got up and went home. When the crowd saw this, they were filled with awe; and they praised God, who had given such authority to men (*NIV*).

C. JESUS IS CALLED THE "SON OF GOD"

"The beginning of the gospel of Jesus Christ, the Son of God" (Mark 1:1). "Then a voice came from heaven, 'You are My beloved Son, in whom I am well pleased'"

Son of God

(1:11). "And who through the Spirit of holiness was declared with power to be the Son of God" (Romans 1:4, *NIV*). "But when the fullness of time had come, God sent forth His Son" (Galatians 4:4).

D. JESUS IS CALLED THE "WORD OF GOD"

"In the beginning was the Word, and the Word was with God, and the Word was God. He was in the beginning with God. All things were made through Him and without Him nothing was made that was made" (John 1:1-3).

It is very important to see from John 1:1-3 that Jesus coexisted with God ("He was in the beginning with God"). God the Father did not create Jesus the Son. They are and have always been coequal, coeternal (as is also true of the Holy Spirit). God the Son is God because He is co-creator of all things ("all things were made through Him").

E. JESUS IS DIRECTLY CALLED "GOD"

"Christ, who is God over all, forever praised! Amen" (Romans 9:5, *NIV*). "The righteousness of our God and Savior Jesus Christ" (2 Peter 1:1).

Other references for study: John 20:28; Acts 2:36; 7:59; Ephesians 1:21.

F. GOD THE HOLY SPIRIT IS GOD

Take time to read the following quotation from Arrington aloud:

> Many scriptures compel us to regard the Holy Spirit as God, coequal with the Father and Son. These same scriptures make it clear that we are to understand the Spirit is a person. He performs personal acts such as teaching (John 14:26), commissioning (Acts 13:2), guiding (Acts 16:6), and interceding (Romans 8:26). He is affected in personal ways. He can be blasphemed (Matthew 12:31, 32) and grieved (Ephesians 4:30). He has intelligence—"the Spirit searches all things, yes, the deep things of God" (1 Corinthians 2:10). He has will—the Spirit distributes spiritual gifts "to each one individually as He wills" (12:11). The Holy Spirit is identified as God. When Ananias lied to the Holy Spirit, Peter declared, "You have not lied to men but to God" (Acts 5:3, 4). In lying to the person of the Holy Spirit, Ananias lied to God (*Christian Doctrine*, 136).

Now, review the scriptures mentioned above and meditate upon the reality of the Holy Spirit as God:

> But the Helper, the Holy Spirit, whom the Father will send in My name, He will teach you all things, and bring to your remembrance all things that I said to you (John 14:26).

> As they ministered to the Lord and fasted, the Holy Spirit said, "Now separate to Me Barnabas and Saul for the work to which I have called them" (Acts 13:2).

> Paul and his companions traveled throughout the region of Phrygia and Galatia, having been kept by the Holy Spirit from preaching the word in the province of Asia (Acts 16:6, *NIV*).

> Then Peter said, "Ananias, how is it that Satan has so filled your heart that you have lied to the Holy Spirit and have kept for yourself some of the money you received for the land? Didn't it belong to you before it was sold? And after it was sold, wasn't the money at your disposal? What made you think of doing such a thing? You have not lied to men but to God (Acts 5:3, 4, *NIV*).

Other references for study: Matthew 12:31, 32; Romans 8:26; Ephesians 4:30; 1 Corinthians 2:10.

LESSON REVIEW

Now, go back to each of the five main points of the lesson:

Five Main Points

- ◈ Declaration of Faith
- ◈ God Is the Model for the Pentecostal Experience
- ◈ The Triune God in the Old Testament
- ◈ The Triune God in the New Testament
- ◈ Three Distinct Persons of the Godhead

Make sure that you have taken time to respond to questions from Applying the Truth/My Daily Walk With God.

Respond

This study should result in each individual and the entire group being brought into personal worship and devotion to the triune God. You may want to sing the hymns and choruses again or think of others which have the Trinity in their message.

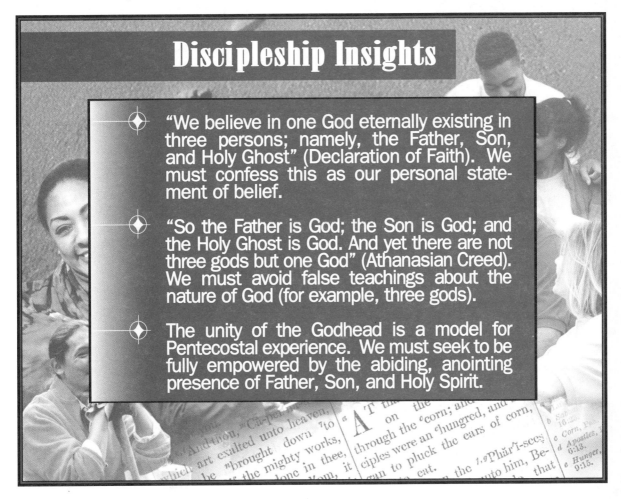

Discipleship Insights

- ◈ "We believe in one God eternally existing in three persons; namely, the Father, Son, and Holy Ghost" (Declaration of Faith). We must confess this as our personal statement of belief.

- ◈ "So the Father is God; the Son is God; and the Holy Ghost is God. And yet there are not three gods but one God" (Athanasian Creed). We must avoid false teachings about the nature of God (for example, three gods).

- ◈ The unity of the Godhead is a model for Pentecostal experience. We must seek to be fully empowered by the abiding, anointing presence of Father, Son, and Holy Spirit.

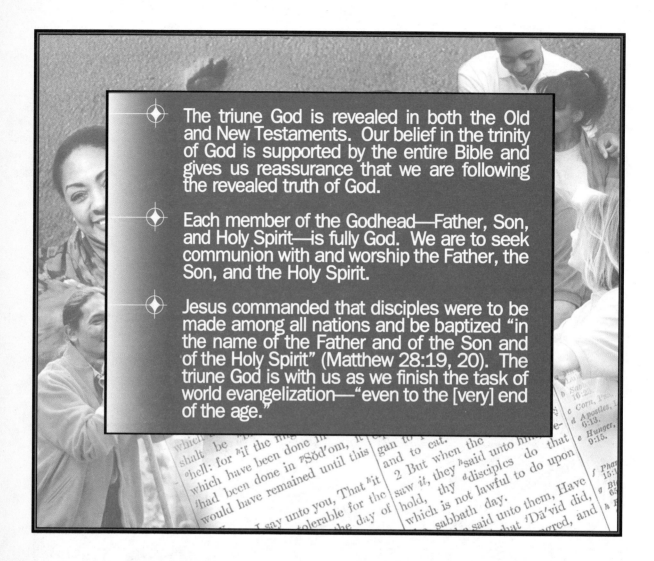

The triune God is revealed in both the Old and New Testaments. Our belief in the trinity of God is supported by the entire Bible and gives us reassurance that we are following the revealed truth of God.

Each member of the Godhead—Father, Son, and Holy Spirit—is fully God. We are to seek communion with and worship the Father, the Son, and the Holy Spirit.

Jesus commanded that disciples were to be made among all nations and be baptized "in the name of the Father and of the Son and of the Holy Spirit" (Matthew 28:19, 20). The triune God is with us as we finish the task of world evangelization—"even to the [very] end of the age."

Resources

Arrington, French L. *Christian Doctrine: A Pentecostal Perspective,* Vol. 1. Cleveland, TN: Pathway Press, 1992.

Duffield, Guy P. and Nathaniel M. VanCleave. *Foundations of Pentecostal Theology.* Los Angeles: L.I.F.E. Bible College, 1983.

Horton, Stanley M., ed. *Systematic Theology: A Pentecostal Perspective.* Springfield, MO: LOGION Press, 1994.

NOTES:_____

_____

_____

_____

JESUS CHRIST

God-Man, the Sacrifice, the Intercessor

LESSON 3

Jerald Daffe

INTRODUCTION

Who Is Jesus?

"Who is Jesus?"

Though first asked nearly 2,000 years ago, this ancient question continues to be a contemporary issue. Its importance can be seen in Christ's discipleship of the Twelve. While ministering in northern Palestine, He asked them first concerning how the people identified Him. He then followed up their answers with a very pointed inquiry: "Who do you say that I am?" (Matthew 16:15).

Let's take a quiz before proceeding any further. Check each of the statements you believe accurately answers the question, "Who is Jesus?"

☐ 1. A good teacher and moral philosopher

☐ 2. A divine miracle worker

☐ 3. A social revolutionary who was executed before being able to bring a political revolution against Rome

☐ 4. God's divine Son who lived on earth without sin

☐ 5. A poor carpenter who became an itinerant preacher and for a while had widespread popularity

☐ 6. A divine being who came and possessed a human body

☐ 7. A liar or lunatic who made fantastic claims about being divine but died like everybody else

Missing the Mark

Each of this wide variety of questions emphasizes an aspect of Christ's life. All of them miss who He really is, and several of them contain error. If you checked answers numbered 2, 4 and 5, you have selected the most accurate statements of the seven; however, they too miss the totality of who Jesus really is. These inadequacies will be seen as you work through the lesson.

How important is it for us as believers to fully grasp the answer to the short question, "Who is Jesus?" Without exaggeration it is the single most important doctrinal issue to be addressed. Our salvation depends not only upon finding but also maintaining the correct answer.

Most Important Doctrine

This lesson will definitely confront you with ideas and concepts which cannot be easily understood with our human abilities. Our finite minds aren't capable of reasoning or seeing how certain items could be so. Therefore, since God's Word declares them to be true, it becomes our responsibility to accept them by faith.

Daily Faith

Keep in mind that we do this in many areas of our lives on a daily basis. We believe, accept and participate in a number of things which we really don't understand. For example, I don't understand how many parts of my car work, but it doesn't stop me from believing in them and more importantly using my car. List some items/things that are true and you believe in but that you don't understand.

_____

_____

_____

_____

_____

Now before going any further, take a few minutes to pray. Ask the Lord to increase your faith and help you believe what the Bible teaches about Jesus Christ and His being both God and man—Jesus, the God-man.

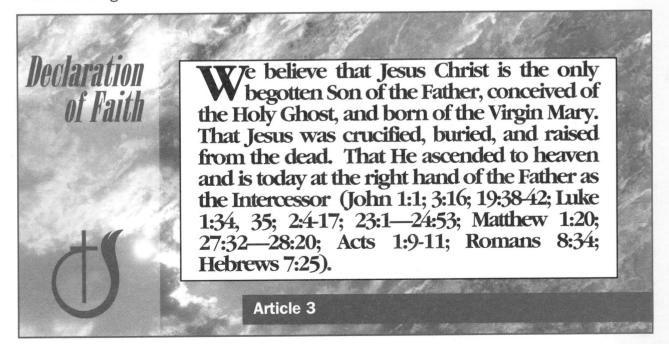

Declaration of Faith

We believe that Jesus Christ is the only begotten Son of the Father, conceived of the Holy Ghost, and born of the Virgin Mary. That Jesus was crucified, buried, and raised from the dead. That He ascended to heaven and is today at the right hand of the Father as the Intercessor (John 1:1; 3:16; 19:38-42; Luke 1:34, 35; 2:4-17; 23:1—24:53; Matthew 1:20; 27:32—28:20; Acts 1:9-11; Romans 8:34; Hebrews 7:25).

Article 3

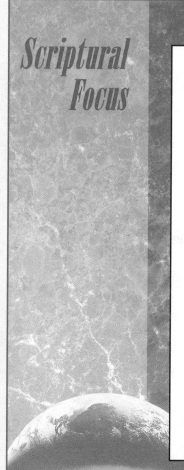

And she shall bring forth a son, and thou shalt call his name JESUS: for he shall save his people from their sins. Now all this was done, that it might be fulfilled which was spoken of the Lord by the prophet, saying, Behold, a virgin shall be with child, and shall bring forth a son, and they shall call his name Emmanuel, which being interpreted is, God with us (Matthew 1:21-23).

And when he had spoken these things, while they beheld, he was taken up; and a cloud received him out of their sight (Acts 1:9).

For I delivered unto you first of all that which I also received, how that Christ died for our sins according to the scriptures; and that he was buried, and that he rose again the third day according to the scriptures (1 Corinthians 15: 3, 4).

Matthew 1:21-23 ✦ Acts 1:9 ✦ 1 Corinthians 15:3, 4

JESUS CHRIST IS THE ONLY BEGOTTEN SON OF THE FATHER

The first sentence of this third article begins with a study of Christ's nature. This includes our understanding of both His divinity and His humanity. Each is vital to a wholesome, Biblical understanding of Jesus.

Christ's Deity

We must, however, begin with Christ's deity and present Him as the Son of God. The apostle John establishes this priority and sets the example for us in the first verse of his Gospel: "In the beginning was the Word, and the Word was with God, and the Word was God." Why is this the beginning point? The answer is simply this: Unless Christ's deity is projected and accepted to begin with, the events of His humanity will not have consistent meaning.

Christ's deity is the most crucial doctrinal issue for us to believe. Without it there is no provision of salvation to bring us into fellowship with God. Unless we believe in Christ's deity, there is no bridge over the gulf of sin which separates us from God. Only One sent from God himself would provide the perfect sacrifice which frees us from sin and the continual need to offer the blood of bulls and goats.

Begotten, Not Created

This first part of the article is taken directly from John 3:16, the golden text of the Bible: "For God so loved the world that He gave His only begotten Son, that whoever believes in Him should not perish but have everlasting life." To begin with, it is important to have a proper understanding of what *begotten* means. First it cannot be viewed in terms of creating. Jesus is not a creation of the Father. This would make Him lesser than God the Father in terms of there being a time in which the Trinity never existed. It would rob Him of possessing all the fullness of God and be in total opposition to Colossians 1:19: "For God was pleased to have all his fullness dwell in him" (*NIV*).

One With the Father

Instead, *begotten* needs to be understood in terms of being His own. It reflects their sameness. The Son is very much God as is the Father. There is no thought of Jesus Christ being like, similar or related to God. But, rather, He is entirely one with God the Father and thus deity. Now you are better able to grasp why you were asked to pray for faith.

If you emphasize reason or have your mind dulled by unbelief, Christ's deity is viewed as mythical, impossible or even highly unreasonable. But on the other hand, when you accept the Bible as the inerrant, authoritative Word of God for today, Christ's deity becomes very obvious. Let's look at some of the Biblical proofs of His deity.

Divine Names

To begin with, one needs to note that the Bible records divine names being given to Jesus. Repeatedly He is called both God and the Son of God. This definitely proclaims His divine nature.

Before going further, read the following proof scriptures:

Matthew 3:17   Titus 2:13   Hebrews 1:8   1 John 5:20

Jesus personally claims to be God. Repeatedly He proclaims this relationship with the Father and accepts this title whenever it is applied to Him. Never does He rebuke anyone or correct their error.

Read the following proof scriptures:

Matthew 11:27; 18:19, 20; 27:40, 43   Mark 14:61, 62

John 14:9-11; 20:21

Personal Testimonies

Consider the personal testimonies of two of the 12 disciples as they proclaim Jesus' deity. Remember Peter. He often speaks too quickly and inaccurately. But when he emphatically states, "You are the Christ, the Son of the living God" (Matthew 16:16), Jesus commends him. And there's Thomas. We remember his doubting. He determines not to believe in Jesus' resurrection until He sees and touches Christ. However, when the resurrected Christ appears in the room, he proclaims, "My Lord and my God!" (John 20:28).

Christ's actions are proof of His deity. These include the acceptance of worship, forgiving sins and performing miracles.

Worship

It would have been pure idolatry for Jesus to accept worship if He wasn't deity. This action would be totally in opposition to the first commandment. No one could be a good teacher and an upright Jew and still allow such actions by His disciples. But Jesus did. (Read Matthew 14:33; 28:9.)

Forgiveness

Plus, He also forgives sin. No wonder the Pharisees charge Him with blasphemy. Since they refuse to accept His deity, they are left with no other choice. But regardless of their opinions, Jesus freely offers forgiveness. Without explanation or apology He forgives the sins of the paralytic who is lowered through the roof for physical healing (Mark 2:1-12). Not to be overlooked is His forgiving of the sins of the woman who washes His feet with her tears and dries them with her hair (Luke 7:36-50).

Miracles

And then there are all those miracles which dramatically demonstrate Christ's deity. They span from raising the dead to healing disease to controlling the power of nature. Neither blind eyes nor stormy seas can withstand His power. Christ's summary of His power is seen in Matthew 28:18 when He states, "All authority has been given to Me in heaven and on earth." Through these miracles Jesus glorifies God, helps needy people and proves the reality of His claims of deity.

Pause here and read the following scriptures:

John 11   Mark 8:1-10   Matthew 8:23-27
Luke 4:38-41; 17:17-19

Applying the Truth
MY DAILY WALK WITH GOD

Answer these questions on the basis of studying this first section on Christ's deity:

What was most difficult for you to believe? _____

_____

_____

What was easier for you to believe? _____

_____

_____

What personal benefit/blessing comes from believing in Christ's

deity? _____

_____

_____

CONCEIVED OF THE HOLY GHOST, AND BORN OF THE VIRGIN MARY

Christ's Humanity

The need for our faith to remain strong even when we can't specifically comprehend continues into this section. Now we must deal with how Jesus, the Son of God, takes on human flesh. Here we will see how two natures—the divine and the human—will reside in one person. One will not dominate over the other. Nor will they combine to create a third or hybrid nature. Instead, they will remain separate, thus enabling us to speak of Jesus Christ as the God-man. Therefore, He is fully God and fully man.

Incarnation

What we are discussing here is referred to as the Incarnation. It simply means that God, in the person of Jesus Christ, took on human flesh and lived as a human being here on earth. His total identification with humanity is seen by following the entire chain of life: conception, development and eventually death.

But to begin with, Christ's taking on human flesh differs from that of our own. He wasn't conceived and birthed through the normal physical union of a man and a woman. First of all, that would have resulted in a person who was totally human. Second, it would have produced a sinful being who could not be the perfect sinless sacrifice for all of humanity. Instead Mary experienced a miraculous conception. The Holy Spirit moved upon her, and she became pregnant without the use of human sperm. This is why we refer to it as the Virgin Birth.

Applying the Truth
MY DAILY WALK WITH GOD

Gospel authors Matthew and Luke are very specific in stating the miraculous circumstances surrounding the conception of Jesus within Mary. Before continuing any further, read the following two scriptures: Matthew 1:20 and Luke 1:35.

What enables you to believe in the Virgin Birth? _____

_____

_____

An equal priority needs to be given to the study of Christ's human nature as well as His divine nature. Without this balance we will have a very limited understanding of what Christ's coming to earth in human form means to each one of us today. His humanity serves two very important purposes.

Historical Jesus

First, a study of Christ's humanity proves that there is a historical Jesus. He did exist here on earth during the first century. Of special importance to our witness and beliefs is the fact of secular historians of that time period including tidbits about Jesus. It served their particular religious beliefs no special purpose, but our having extra-Biblical sources furthers the truth of what we believe. Jesus is no myth dreamed up by someone trying to pull a religious hoax!

Jesus stands forth as a man who lived on this earth. This enables Him to be known in terms of His family and His followers. And as would be expected, He follows the cultural patterns of His ethnic group.

Human Characteristics

Second, a study of Christ's humanity indicates His being subject to the weaknesses and temptations which are common to all humans. This enables Him to identify with us. He really does know how we feel!

The Bible reveals Jesus' humanity in a number of ways, thus fully supporting the reality of His being human.

Let's return to His human parentage as indicated in the article of faith. Jesus develops in Mary's womb in the exact same manner as any other human who is born. Mary was His birth mother, not an adopted mother. Throughout the Scriptures, Mary is referred to as Jesus' mother.

Human Parentage

Read the following scriptures indicating His human parentage:

Matthew 1:18-25   Luke 2:5-7

John 2:1-5   Galatians 4:4

Notice the common developmental process of Jesus. Except for the one brief glimpse of Christ's being in the Temple at age 12, we know very little of His childhood and early manhood. However, Luke provides us with one small insight which indicates His following the pattern of growth and development like any other Jewish boy (2:52).

Human Appearance

Christ's appearance and form also serve to emphasize His humanity. The Samaritan woman recognized Jesus as a Jew. Surely this means His hair color, eyes, skin pigmentation and facial features reflected Jewish parentage. Not to be forgotten was the disciples' recognition of Jesus after the Resurrection. This must indicate the retention of facial features by which they had known Him.

Human Needs

Of special importance is the fact of Jesus' being vulnerable to the same physical needs and range of emotions as all human beings. Because of His two natures being separate from each other, He wasn't a superman who transcended fatigue, hunger, thirst, pain and sorrow.

Read the following scriptures which share the previous aspect of His humanity:

Matthew 4:2; 14:13; 26:36-40

Luke 8:23, 24

Mark 4:38; 15:41

John 4:7; 11:35; 19:28

Applying the Truth

MY DAILY WALK WITH GOD

Read Hebrews 4:14-16 and then answer the following:

Which of my struggles does Jesus understand? _____

_____

Which of my temptations does Jesus understand? _____

_____

_____

Why should I be able to pray with greater confidence as I present

my weaknesses and temptations to the Lord? _____

_____

_____

Two Natures

Having completed the first two areas of discussion, we can Biblically see the divine and human natures of Jesus. The question which needs to be properly answered is, "How do these two natures operate within the same person?" The danger which occurs now, and which occurred during the centuries, is that of overemphasizing one nature at the expense of the other. And when one of them is minimized or maximized, we strip Christ of His true identity and ministry.

Christ isn't a split personality in which each one of the natures takes turns dominating or being publicly evident. Instead they continually operate in unity and harmony. Neither one governs or overshadows the other.

JESUS WAS CRUCIFIED, BURIED AND RAISED FROM THE DEAD

Why did Jesus come to this earth?

Why He Came

One verse from the Gospel of Mark immediately comes to mind: "For even the Son of Man did not come to be served, but to serve, and to give His life a ransom for many" (10:45).

The first part of this verse emphasizes what we describe as His active ministry—Jesus the doer. It's this dimension of His three-year ministry that receives the greatest coverage in the Gospels. This centers around the four major areas of preaching, teaching, discipleship and miracles. All of them are continuous throughout

Jesus' short ministry in the limited area of Palestine. His principle of ministry in these areas may be summarized by "I must work the works of Him who sent Me, while it is day; the night is coming when no one can work" (John 9:4).

Though Christ's active ministry isn't part of this article of the Declaration of Faith, it deserves a brief review.

Preaching

When Jesus stood up in the synagogue at Nazareth, read from Isaiah, and then stated it was fulfilled in Himself, His work of preaching was projected. This emphasis on preaching is seen when sending out the 12 disciples on their first mission outreach. They were to follow His example and preach.

Read the following scriptures on Jesus' preaching:

Isaiah 61:1, 2   Luke 4:16-19; 9:1-6

Matthew 10:5-7

Teaching

Christ's extensive teaching becomes very evident when reading the Gospels. In fact, nearly three-fifths of Matthew's Gospel is comprised of His teaching discoveries. Of special interest is the relevance of what was said to their daily lives and their perception of the authority with which He spoke!

Read these scriptures on Jesus' teaching:

Matthew 4:23; 5:1, 2; 7:29   Luke 4:15; 11:1

John 7:14-17; 14:23

Discipleship

Twelve chosen men are Christ's constant companions during His ministry. He invests of Himself in them through personal example, public discussion and private conferences. They stand beside Him in triumph and in crisis. Along with this initial group of disciples, He takes time to send out 70 others.

Read the listed scriptures on Jesus' discipleship:

Matthew 10; 18:1 ff.   Mark 3:13-19; 9:28-32

Luke 10; 11:1 ff.   John 6:60-71; 16:1-4

Miracles

Spread throughout the four Gospels are 35 specific miracles as well as the indication of many more. Several passages state that Christ healed all who were ill. This means we have no way of estimating the number of miracles performed. However, we do know they cover a wide cross-section of human need—multitudes fed, blinded eyes opened, atrophic limbs restored and the dead raised.

Applying the Truth
MY DAILY WALK WITH GOD

As Christ's disciples we are to follow His example. That includes serving others. What are some ways that you can be of service to others?

◈ Family Members? _____	
_____	
◈ Neighbors? _____	
_____	
_____	
◈ Fellow Believers? _____	
_____	
_____	

His Passive Mission

The second aspect of Mark 10:45 deals specifically with Christ's passive mission—others doing to Him. This is the major reason for Christ's coming to earth. Death was a definite part of Christ's work here. He made a definite choice to accept a fate which He could have chosen to avoid.

If it were not for this aspect of Christ's ministry, all of His other humanitarian actions would have been of very limited benefit. Without Christ's death there would be no salvation. Christianity and our faith would be like all the other religions of the world. There would be a founder, a set of rules and teachings, but no access to God.

Crucifixion

Christ's death isn't the result of illegal revolutionary actions or being a martyr for a noble cause. But rather it is a distinct, preplanned part of His total ministry. He came to die the death of crucifixion. The plan of salvation includes His suffering a degrading, humiliating, agonizing death reserved for rebels and criminals. Though sinless, He takes on our sins that we might be free to inherit eternal life.

Read these selected scriptures on Christ's dying:

Psalm 22:1, 8	Matthew 16:21	Mark 8:31-33
Luke 9:22	John 3:14, 15	Romans 3:23-25
Hebrews 9:26		

Resurrection

How wonderful that the story doesn't end with Christ's body being placed in another man's grave! This takes us to a third dimension of Christ's ministry—His resurrection. It provides us with a central or fundamental doctrine. Here we have a dynamic which cannot be found in any other religion or belief system.

Christ's resurrection is of vital importance to all of us. Without His rising from the dead we would still be steeped in sin and hopelessness. Without the Resurrection we would have no hope of being resurrected from the dead and living eternally.

Read these uplifting scriptures on Christ's resurrection:

Mark 16:6	Luke 24:6-8	John 20:5-7
Romans 4:25	1 Peter 1:3	Revelation 1:18

Ascension

Forty days after Christ's resurrection He ascended to heaven. It was a marvelous experience for those disciples who were present. Two angelic beings appeared and restated Jesus' promise of returning. In response the believers worshiped and then returned into the city of Jerusalem in a spirit of joy and expectation (Acts 1:9-12).

Christ's ascension signaled the beginning of His ministry of intercession in heaven for us.

Intercession

This aspect receives little Scriptural discussion; however, there are two direct Scripture references which are more than sufficient (Romans 8:34; Hebrews 7:25). Each already states that from His ascension to the present, Christ is in heaven interceding on our behalf.

This really is a continuation of His ministry here on earth. John 17 records Jesus' prayer as He intercedes for His disciples and for all believers. He prays very specifically for their protection, sanctification, unity and eventual glorification.

Assurance

What does His intercessory work mean to each of us? Most importantly, it provides wonderful assurance for every believer. He is our security. We know there is an Advocate before the heavenly Father pleading in our behalf. He constantly seeks for our spiritual and physical protection in accord with God's will.

Applying the Truth
MY DAILY WALK WITH GOD

How does Christ's sacrificial death impact your love for Him and your desire to worship Him? _____

_____

_____

_____

_____

_____

_____

How does knowing of Christ's intercessory work encourage you in your prayer life? _____

_____

_____

_____

_____

LESSON REVIEW

Jesus Christ, the Son of God, came to earth and assumed human flesh. Though fully God and fully man, these two natures remained separate, thus enabling Him to be the God-man.

The miraculous combination of deity and humanity is accomplished by a miraculous conception in the Virgin Mary through the ministry of the Holy Spirit.

Christ's major purpose for coming to earth was to be the sacrifice for our sins. His resurrection gives us hope for the future.

We have an Advocate before our heavenly Father through the intercessory work of Jesus Christ.

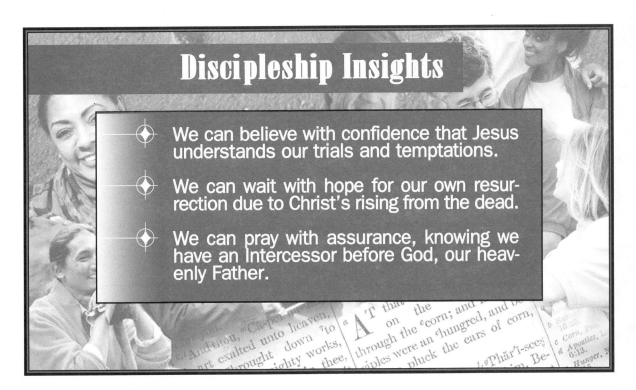

Discipleship Insights

- We can believe with confidence that Jesus understands our trials and temptations.

- We can wait with hope for our own resurrection due to Christ's rising from the dead.

- We can pray with assurance, knowing we have an Intercessor before God, our heavenly Father.

Resources

Arrington, French L. *Christian Doctrine: A Pentecostal Perspective, Vol. 2.* Cleveland, TN: Pathway Press, 1993.

Bloesch, Donald G. *Essentials of Evangelical Theology,* Vol. 1, *God, Authority and Salvation.* San Francisco: Harper and Row Publication, 1978.

Bruce, F.F. *Jesus: Lord and Savior.* Downer's Grove, IL: Intervarsity Press, 1986.

Morris, Leon. *The Atonement: Its Meaning and Significance.* Downer's Grove, IL: Intervarsity Press, 1983.

NOTES:_____

_____

_____

_____

_____

_____

_____

_____

_____

_____

_____

_____

_____

_____

_____

_____

_____

_____

REPENTANCE

Call to Repentance

Oliver McMahan

LESSON 4

INTRODUCTION

Abuse and Pain

    I remember ministering at a hospital to a woman who had been physically abused. Her eyes pierced through any thought of happiness. Pain welled up around her eyelids and pulsated the tale of tragic abuse. How could anyone be so cruel as to injure another human being? The footprints of sin are all too clear when you look at the trail of pain left in their wake. Where do we discover the sins that beset us all? Peering into the human soul is difficult. I didn't want to look too long into the eyes of the woman I saw in the hospital that day who had been abused by someone else. I didn't want to look too long because her eyes played the tape of the sins that ran the breadth from society to each solitary individual. The inventory of each of our hearts and the imperfections that blot the soul cried out through that woman's tears.

Call to Repentance

    Tragedy permeates our society and blame covers us all. "But I haven't brutalized anyone," an innocent bystander might comment. However, looking into the eyes of Christ, I see perfection as well as pain and realize that in the gaze of the Savior is the clear call to repent—to repent of all my sin . . . to remove all the tragedy . . . to return to the only One who can set us free!

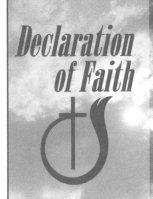

Declaration of Faith

We believe that all have sinned and come short of the glory of God and that repentance is commanded of God for all and necessary for forgiveness of sins (Mark 1:15; Luke 13:3; Acts 3:19).

Article 4

Scriptural Focus

And immediately, coming up from the water, He saw the heavens parting and the Spirit descending upon Him like a dove. Then a voice came from heaven, "You are My beloved Son, in whom I am well pleased." Immediately the Spirit drove Him into the wilderness. And He was there in the wilderness forty days, tempted by Satan, and was with the wild beasts; and the angels ministered to Him. Now after John was put in prison, Jesus came to Galilee, preaching the gospel of the kingdom of God, and saying, "The time is fulfilled, and the kingdom of God is at hand. Repent, and believe in the gospel." And as He walked by the Sea of Galilee, He saw Simon and Andrew his brother casting a net into the sea; for they were fishermen. Then Jesus said to them, "Follow Me, and I will make you become fishers of men."

Mark 1:10-17

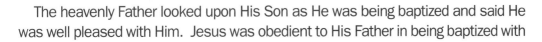

REPENTANCE IS ABOUT JESUS

The heavenly Father looked upon His Son as He was being baptized and said He was well pleased with Him. Jesus was obedient to His Father in being baptized with water. Obedience drew the ovation of the Almighty. Coming from the warmth of the embrace of the Father was also the drive of the Spirit to test the obedient heart of Jesus by sending Him into the wilderness of sin's temptation. He would be exposed to the cruelest of accusations, from the father of all accusers. In the wilderness, the father of sin would search the sincerity of the Savior.

Defeating Sin

Bursting out of the wilderness came Jesus, conquering every sin, even the original crafter of sin himself. The embodiment of obedience had defeated the personifier of sin. The news was that the heavenly Father's Son had won over the rebellious tempter.

Clothed in perfect, mighty, victorious righteousness, Christ broke out of the wilderness declaring, "Return from your sins! Come back to the Father. The tempter is defeated. He can do you no harm. Leave, for He cannot cleave to your soul. No matter what the father of liars says, he has no claim on you!"

The Kingdom Is Near

There is Jesus. Can you see Him? He's coming out of the wilderness, leading you and me away from our sins. The sight of Him is matched by the sound of His voice: "Repent of your sin. The time is fulfilled; the kingdom of God is at hand!" Jesus is the reason to repent. Our sins are exposed by His faithfulness to the Father. Christ came out of the wilderness so we might come out of our sin. No matter what the devil has told you about your sin, Christ is telling you that you can be free and obedient to the heavenly Father.

Help for the Helpless

I desperately wanted to help the woman I met that day—sitting there in the corridor, holding on to a wheelchair, letting no one touch her pain as she sat under an avalanche of human shame. What screams accompanied the blows that came upon her? Who could have stopped the abuser? Who could have stopped her pain? I wanted to tell her of One who had walked through the same valley of death that she had been thrown into. But I knew that in that hallway no word I could say would reach her tears, and fears, like the call of the wilderness Savior.

REPENTANCE IS ABOUT US

Sin's Temptation

Jesus came out of the wilderness of sin's temptation directly to each one of us. The countryside of Judea that Jesus walked is matched today by the skyscraper, the suburb, the sanctuary of our hearts. He steps into our lives because His confrontation with the tempter was not for His own cause but His compassion for us.

The Call to Repent

Walking by each of us is the Savior. He stops and calls our name. "Will you repent? Will you come after Me into the kingdom of My Father?" You are the reason He broke open the way of repentance. "Repent!" is a call, not a cause. The call is to you, not someone beside you. You are the reason. "Repent!" is on His lips as He walks among us.

Repentance is the cry when we see the pain inflicted by sin. Sin will cease when we respond to the Prince of Peace who endured great conflict and temptation so that we might repent of our sin. I had not abused the woman; I did know her abuser. But if anything was to stop the sin of shameful abuse, the turning of the hand that had stricken her, it would come only from the abuser responding to the call of the wilderness Savior. Out of the wilderness of sin came One who calls, "Repent!"

Applying the Truth
MY DAILY WALK WITH GOD

In your prayer time, pray that you would hear the call of Christ. Begin with the sins that you know you have committed and have yet to repent of. Look at those sins as temptations that you have given in to. Then, focus on the reality that Christ has walked through that temptation and calls you to repent and be free of the tempter's lies. Take the following steps:

◆ Confess temptations that you have encountered.

◆ Pray, knowing that Christ has already walked through victorious over that temptation.

◆ Repent of your sin and of your compromise to temptation.

◆ Follow Jesus in His victory over temptation and sin.

Scriptural Focus

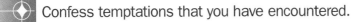

There were present at that season some who told Him about the Galileans whose blood Pilate had mingled with their sacrifices. And Jesus answered and said to them, "Do you suppose that these Galileans were worse sinners than all other Galileans, because they suffered such things? "I tell you, no; but unless you repent you will all likewise perish. "Or those eighteen on whom the tower in Siloam fell and killed them, do you think that they were worse sinners than all other men who dwelt in Jerusalem? "I tell you, no; but unless you repent you will all likewise perish."

Luke 13:1-5

CALLING YOU, CALLING ME,
CALLING EVERY ONE OF US

The Need of Repentance

Still saying, "I have no need to repent"? "But I haven't brutalized or abused anyone," still your confession? Remember the woman in the corridor that I saw. I can't forget her. And yes, I thought at first, *Who could do such a thing!* But then, the call of the Savior said to me that even though my sin was not abuse, I still needed to repent. Repentance is not relative to sin. Repentance is regulated by the Savior. Jesus was listening to good people that day when they reminded Him of the horror of blood sacrifice and human brutality. Jesus' response? "You repent." If only the chiefest of sinners must repent, then the smallest of sins would flourish, even within good people. Sin is no "respecter of persons". The smallest cell of sin will canker the entire body. Jesus said, "Repent!" because the seed is as lethal as the tree.

 THE ALTERNATIVE

Two Alternatives

The bargaining table of repentance is narrow. You really have only two choices: Repent or perish. Choose not to repent of any sin in your life and you perish. No intermediate step, no preliminary proving stage and certainly no alternatives. "But I don't want to perish," you might say. Sorry! Your choice not to repent is your choice to perish. The call to repentance works like that. Your response is your decision. Alternative one—repent. Failure to exercise that option automatically defaults you to alternative two—perish.

Repent or Perish

In Luke 13:1-5, Jesus repeated the call to repentance and its alternative. He said, "Unless you repent you will all likewise perish" (vv. 3, 5). Repenting—repenting now—is that important! While I am gazing at another person's sin, Christ is pointing out my own sin. While the echoes of my complaints about the sins of others are still ringing across the room, the call of Christ convicts me of my own sins against others.

Applying the Truth
MY DAILY WALK WITH GOD

As you pray, ask yourself not only about the impact and degree of the sins of others but also about your own sin. There is a certain kind of temptation to pray, asking God to do something about what others are doing without asking God about what I am to do. Answer the following questions, true or false, to probe your own need to heed the call to repent.

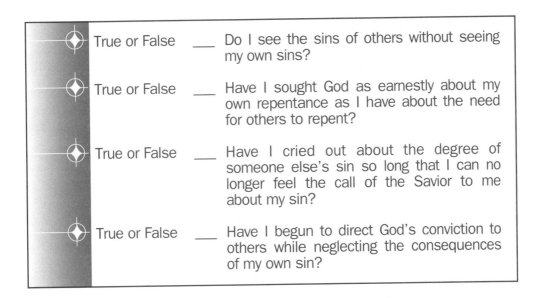

◆ True or False	___	Do I see the sins of others without seeing my own sins?
◆ True or False	___	Have I sought God as earnestly about my own repentance as I have about the need for others to repent?
◆ True or False	___	Have I cried out about the degree of someone else's sin so long that I can no longer feel the call of the Savior to me about my sin?
◆ True or False	___	Have I begun to direct God's conviction to others while neglecting the consequences of my own sin?

Scriptural Focus

So when Peter saw it, he responded to the people: "Men of Israel, why do you marvel at this? Or why look so intently at us, as though by our own power or godliness we had made this man walk? The God of Abraham, Isaac, and Jacob, the God of our fathers, glorified His Servant Jesus, whom you delivered up and denied in the presence of Pilate, when he was determined to let Him go. . . . Yet now, brethren, I know that you did it in ignorance, as did also your rulers. But those things which God foretold by the mouth of all His prophets, that the Christ would suffer, He has thus fulfilled. Repent therefore and be converted, that your sins may be blotted out, so that times of refreshing may come from the presence of the Lord, the Lord."

Acts 3:12, 13, 17-19

What About Jesus?

Repentance is not just a question of "What shall I do with my sins?" The real, wake-up question is, "What shall I do with Jesus?" You're not just deciding how to handle your own life when you decide about repentance. The management of repentance is your response to the Master. The call to repent comes from Him. When you finally decide about repentance, you have to give your answer to Him. He asked the questions, "Will you respond to Me? Will you repent?" He is listening for the answers to these questions. Repentance is not a religious issue; it is a response to Christ's invitation.

Beyond Healing

Peter was grieved that day. A man who had been lame all his life, who was being carried to the Temple gate called Beautiful, had just been healed. The risen Savior had just performed a miracle. As the crowd at the Temple rushed to see the man —for everyone of them had passed by him day after day—Peter was looking beyond joy. The same crowd that had jeered the Savior on the cross now wanted to be joyful on the heels of a miracle. Peter cried out, "Repent!" The same Jesus whom they had refused to hear was the same Jesus who had now revived the limbs of the lame man. Peter was letting them know that they could not reject the Savior and still receive His joy.

Receive Christ

Peter was declaring to the crowd that if they were to fully know and understand what was happening to the man who had been lame, they must repent! Repentance brings the full reality of the Savior. Repentance is not just the turning over of our sins. It is the One to whom we turn them over who makes all the difference. The act of repentance is the act of receiving Christ.

TIMES OF REPENTANCE, TIMES OF REFRESHING

Refreshing

The times of repentance and the times of refreshing are the same. Peter cried out about both realities, "Repent . . . so that the times of refreshing may come" (Acts 3:19). Refreshing was exemplified in the healing of the lame man. His limbs that had once been lifeless were now pulsating with the refreshing, life-giving flow of Christ's healing. Peter was declaring that the life-giving flow in the limbs of the man who had been lame was received through repentance.

Empowered

When we repent of our sins, the Lord brings life to us. Rather than perishing, we live! Instead of being defeated, we rejoice! Instead of being bound, we praise! Repentance is not just remorse over sin, it is receiving the Savior and entering into His life. Repentance is empowerment. The repentant are the walking and leaping! A skeptical, unrepentant world can only run and gaze at the wonders of the Lord. But a repentant heart is catapulted into the arms of the Savior. Not an onlooker, but a new creation! Not just a participator, but a privileged recipient!

Applying the Truth
MY DAILY WALK WITH GOD

Move in your prayer past the vale of observation to the room of receptivity. The Savior is already calling you to repentance. "But I haven't sinned," you might say. Ask the Lord to search your heart. Through the Spirit, listen to His voice, for He may be calling you in ways that can only be heard as you listen closer to Him. In your meditations before the Lord, don't just look on things as you would like to see them. Through the doorway of repentance, enter into the refreshing of the Lord. What is the work of the Lord for you right now? The call to repent is the call to be empowered by the work that He is doing in you right now.

Write out the manner in which the Lord has revealed to you that you need to repent. _____

_____

_____

_____

In what areas have you felt the Lord drawing you toward Himself but you have not quite been able to reach that place? _____

_____

_____

_____

Now, as you repent of those areas that God has called you to repent of, begin to receive the promised refreshing that comes with repentance. The lame man leaped before the Lord; how has God given you renewal and rejoicing as a result of your repentance?

_____

_____

_____

_____

In this lesson you have learned about the call to repent. Jesus calls every one of us to repent, regardless of what we have done or not done. The call comes from His victory over the tempter and accuser. The repentant heart is a heart that follows Christ in victory. The repentant heart is a rejoicing heart. The repentant heart is an empowered soul.

The first tragedy of not repenting is in rejecting Jesus. The second tragedy of not repenting is that the unrepentant heart shall perish. This lesson has asked you to search your own heart in different ways and to turn your heart in prayer to Jesus' call to repent. The lesson has also been a call to decide which you will choose—to repent or to perish.

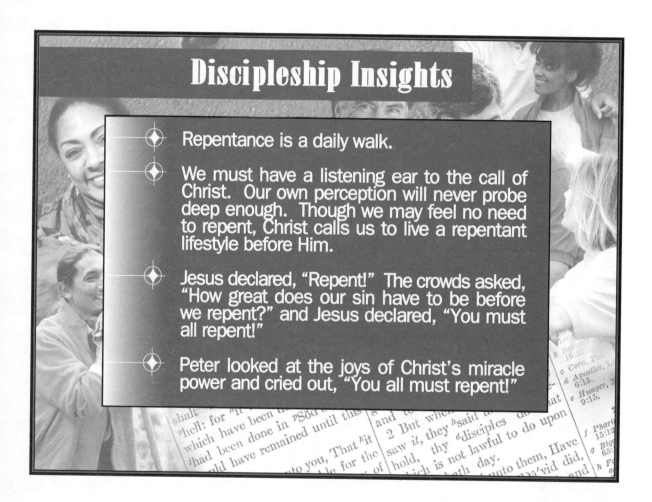

Discipleship Insights

- Repentance is a daily walk.

- We must have a listening ear to the call of Christ. Our own perception will never probe deep enough. Though we may feel no need to repent, Christ calls us to live a repentant lifestyle before Him.

- Jesus declared, "Repent!" The crowds asked, "How great does our sin have to be before we repent?" and Jesus declared, "You must all repent!"

- Peter looked at the joys of Christ's miracle power and cried out, "You all must repent!"

Resources

Arrington, French L. *Christian Doctrine: A Pentecostal Perspective*, Vol. 2. Cleveland, TN: Pathway Press, 1993.

Bloesch, Donald G. *Essentials of Evangelical Theology*, Vol. 2, *Life, Ministry and Hope*. San Francisco: Harper and Row Publishers, 1979.

Bowdle, Donald N. *Redemption Accomplished and Applied*. Cleveland, TN: Pathway Press, 1972.

Gause, Hollis. L. *Living in the Spirit: The Way of Salvation*. Cleveland, TN: Pathway Press, 1980.

Henry, Carl F. H. *God, Revelation and Authority,* Vols. 1-4. Waco, TX: Word Books Publishers, 1983.

Williams, J. Rodman. *Renewal Theology: Salvation, the Holy Spirit, and Christian Living*. Grand Rapids: Zondervan Publishing House, 1990.

NOTES:_____

_____

_____

_____

_____

_____

_____

_____

_____

_____

_____

_____

_____

_____

_____

_____

_____

_____

_____

_____

JUSTIFICATION

The Believer and the Blood

David M. Griffis

INTRODUCTION

Shedding of Blood

God's first interaction with the human race regarding sin and redemption is portrayed in Genesis 3:9-24. Foremost among the objects seen in this Biblical lesson is blood. Blood is found when God slew animals to make coats of skin to cover Adam's and Eve's nakedness. The Bible clearly states that "life . . . is in the blood" (Leviticus 17:11). God is adamant in His requirement for redemption—for sin to be remitted there must be the shedding of blood. Hebrews 9:22 emphatically states, "Without shedding of blood there is no remission."

Declaration of Faith

We believe in justification, regeneration, and the new birth are wrought by faith in the blood of Jesus Christ (Romans 5:1; Titus 3: 5, 7; John 3:3; 1 Peter 1:23; 1 John 3:9).

Article 5

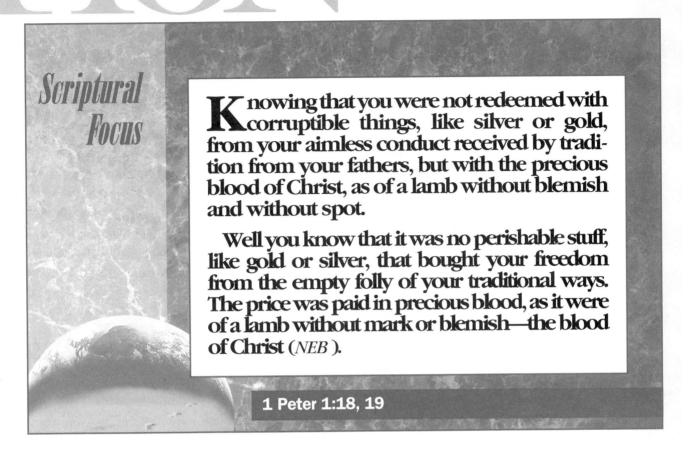

Knowing that you were not redeemed with corruptible things, like silver or gold, from your aimless conduct received by tradition from your fathers, but with the precious blood of Christ, as of a lamb without blemish and without spot.

Well you know that it was no perishable stuff, like gold or silver, that bought your freedom from the empty folly of your traditional ways. The price was paid in precious blood, as it were of a lamb without mark or blemish—the blood of Christ (*NEB*).

1 Peter 1:18, 19

Ritual

In the Old Testament, Israel was taught that blood sacrifice was a covering for sin and a cleansing agent for the human condition. Millions of animals were slain throughout the history of Israel. All this bloodletting was done under the Mosaic Law and in accordance with God's redemptive covenant with His people. The problem was that while God's intention for the people in this blood covenant was to provide forgiveness and holiness, the shedding of blood eventually became simply a ritual for the Israelites.

Escape

However, if one looks at Exodus 12 and sees the portrait painted of Israel in Egyptian bondage and the deliverance that came as a result of the slaying of the Passover lamb, it is easy to understand the great lesson God taught Israel and the human race—escape from bondage must come through the shedding of blood.

Bitter Bondage

Israel's sojourn into Egypt had been intended to prevent annihilation by famine, and they were greatly blessed as a result of the righteousness of Joseph, who had gained the favor of Pharaoh. However, after Joseph's death the Egyptian rulers viewed the increasing numbers of Israelites in the land of Goshen as a threat to Egypt's political stability and strength. Pharaoh felt that the only way to control the Israelites was to enslave them. So Israel was subjected to 400 years of bitter bondage.

Protected by the Blood

God called an 80-year-old shepherd out of the wilderness of Midian to be Israel's deliverer. Pharaoh was a very stubborn individual, resolute in his determination not to let the Israelites go free from bondage. It took many plagues and disasters of unprecedented proportion to get Pharaoh's attention and cause him to understand that Israel's God was the true God. The final plague that came upon Egypt was the death of the firstborn of every household in the land. The only homes that escaped this horrible death plague were those protected by blood.

God's Plan for Salvation

God instituted the Passover, which would remain a time of celebration throughout Israel's history. The Passover was also a futuristic portrait of the Messiah, the Redeemer, and God's Lamb who was to come and deliver people from the bondage of sin. God's instructions to the people of Israel were plain. They were to slay a lamb—a male of the first year, spotless and without blemish—and catch his blood in a basin. Then they were to dip a feathery hyssop plant in the blood and strike the sides of the doorposts and the lintels of each house. When the death angel flew over Egypt at midnight, wherever he saw the blood he would not come into that house. Israel was saved from the plague by the blood. The stubbornness of Pharaoh was broken by the power of the death plague, and Israel was delivered from Egyptian bondage because of the blood.

Symbol of the Redeemer

The sacrificial system as taught to Israel through Moses in the wilderness was a type shadow and symbol of the Redeemer who would come to eradicate the power of sin. The holy prophets had prophesied of such a Redeemer, and a remnant in Israel anxiously awaited this Messiah's arrival.

Forgetting the Blood

God spoke to Israel through Isaiah the prophet and said, "There shall come forth a Rod from the stem of Jesse, and a Branch shall grow out of his roots. The Spirit of the Lord shall rest upon Him, the Spirit of wisdom and understanding, the Spirit of counsel and might, the Spirit of knowledge and of the fear of the Lord" (11:1, 2). But the majority of Israel largely ignored this prophecy because they had become engrossed in the ritualistic practice of sacrifice and forgot or disdained the true meaning of this blood sacrifice. God became very angry because of their ritualism and once again spoke to Israel through Isaiah: "To what purpose is the multitude of your sacrifices to Me? says the Lord. "I have had enough of burnt offerings of rams and the fat of fed cattle. I do not delight in the blood of bulls, or of lambs or goats'" (1:11). God was expressing His anger over ritualistic religion that did not affect the heart. The blood of animals was powerless to change the human heart, and hearts must be changed to justify men before God.

Wounded for Transgressions

The coming of Christ, the true Passover Lamb, would change all that. The purpose of His coming is embodied in the great Isaiah 53 passage of the Suffering Servant, who would be "wounded for our transgressions and bruised for our iniquities." This Servant would come "as a lamb led to the slaughter, and as a sheep dumb before its shearers He would not open His mouth" (see vv. 5:7).

Let us look at what the Bible teaches us concerning the power of the shed blood of Christ to the true believer.

THE BLOOD OF CHRIST CLEANSES FROM ALL UNRIGHTEOUSNESS

The human heart is "desperately wicked" (Jeremiah 17:9). "All have sinned and fall short of the glory of God" (Romans 3:23). "The wages of sin is death" (Romans 6:23). "The soul who sins, shall die" (Ezekiel 18:4). "When lust hath conceived, it bringeth forth sin: and sin, when it is finished, bringeth forth death" (James 1:15, KJV).

These warnings concerning the consequences of sin are awesome and terrible to consider. However, in the midst of the fact that sin produces death both physically and eternally, there is great hope in the fact that the shed blood of Jesus Christ cleanses from all unrighteousness. John's first epistle gives us dramatic proof of this hope. In 1 John 1:7 we read, "But if we walk in the light as He is in the light, we have fellowship with one another, and the blood of Jesus Christ His Son cleanses us from all sin." Verse 9 says, "If we confess our sins, He is faithful and just to forgive us our sins and to cleanse us from all unrighteousness."

As has been previously stated, God will not remit sin without the shedding of blood. The shedding of animal blood had only been a portrait of things that were to come. Jesus Christ was considered by God to be the perfect sacrifice. His sacrifice of blood was perfect enough to be accepted by God to cleanse every repentant sinner from his/her sin.

In our opening Scriptural Focus, the apostle Peter reminded us that perishable things could not redeem our sin. Earthly things such as silver and gold have no power to purchase man's pardon for his sin. Peter said the precious blood of Christ and that alone redeemed us from the corruption of our sin. The word that Peter used, *precious*, means "invaluable, impossible to evaluate as to its true value." So is the precious blood of Christ. Silver and gold could not buy man's redemption. Silver and gold would not cause God to turn His head from the sin and pardon the transgressor. God is not impressed with earthly riches. However, His Son coming to earth and taking on the form of sinful flesh and then giving His life as a ransom for the sins of men was enough to cause God to pardon men of their sin when they believe on His Son as their Savior and Lord.

ILLUSTRATION

The story of the great songwriter William Cowper is the story of the power of the blood of Christ. William Cowper was a very wicked and evil Englishman. His life was one of total failure and destitution. He was on a journey to kill himself one night when he stopped at a small storefront church to warm himself from England's winter. In that storefront church Cowper heard a message preached on the power of the blood of Christ, and this derelict sinner that night surrendered his heart to Jesus Christ, and the blood of Christ washed his sins away. He later wrote the immortal words, "There is a fountain filled with blood / Drawn from Immanuel's veins; / And sinners, plunged beneath that flood, / Lose all their guilty stains." William Cowper's heart must have been deeply moved when he wrote the words to the second verse of that song, which simply said, "The dying thief rejoiced to see / That fountain in his day; / And there may I, though vile as he, / Wash all my sins away."

Sin and Death

Cleansing

Perfect Sacrifice

Precious Blood

Power in the Blood

Applying the Truth

MY DAILY WALK WITH GOD

⬥ Why did God require the shedding of blood for the remission of sin? _____

_____ Why was

⬥ Christ's blood considered to be holy blood? _____

_____

_____

⬥ Why was it important for the Redeemer to be born of a virgin and to be sinless? _____

_____

_____

⬥ If the blood of Christ cleanses from all unrighteousness, then is it not true that salvation by works is futile? _____

_____

_____

THE BLOOD OF CHRIST SANCTIFIES BELIEVERS AND MAKES THEM HOLY BEFORE GOD

Sanctify

The word *sanctify* is translated from a Greek word that means "to make holy." The Bible teaches that we are sanctified through the blood, the Word and the Spirit. In Hebrews 13:12, the Bible teaches that Jesus shed His blood for the sanctification of the people. His suffering was for their holiness.

When Jesus prayed for His disciples, He told the Father, "Sanctify them by Your truth. Your word is truth" (John 17:17). The apostle Paul taught that the Gentiles were acceptable because they were being "sanctified by the Holy Spirit" (Romans 15:16). These three agencies—the blood, the Word and the Spirit—are involved in the sanctification of the believer.

Therefore Jesus also, that He might sanctify the people with His own blood, suffered outside the gate.

Hebrews 13:12

Blood

Notice how these agencies each play a different role in the sanctification or the process of becoming holy. The blood provides for the instantaneous powerful redemptive sanctification of the human heart. This is God's acceptable sacrifice. This is the covering that causes God to pass over the individual and prevent destruction. The Word is a teacher that causes the believer to learn how to be holy, how to act, and how to react. The Word teaches the principles and the truths of the heart of God and imparts sanctification to the mind and to the character of the human being.

Word

The Holy Spirit sanctifies by a subduing of the human spirit to the will of God. The Spirit warns, instructs, guides and leads. That is why the Bible teaches, "For as many as are led by the Spirit of God, these are sons of God" (Romans 8:14).

Spirit

It is important for us to understand that the blood plays a vital role in our sanctification. Jesus knew this when He gave His life on Calvary. The writer of Hebrews says that He was willing to suffer for our sanctification, to cleanse us and to make us whole (see 13:12).

Applying the Truth
MY DAILY WALK WITH GOD

What are the three agencies that enable me to be a sanctified vessel before God? _____

_____

_____

What role does the blood of Christ play in my sanctification?

_____

_____

In the light of how Jesus prayed in John 17, how important is it for me to read my Bible daily? _____

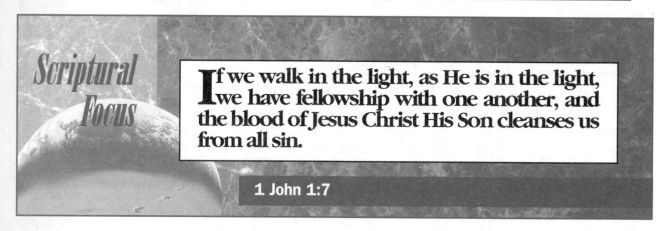

Scriptural Focus

If we walk in the light, as He is in the light, we have fellowship with one another, and the blood of Jesus Christ His Son cleanses us from all sin.

1 John 1:7

THE BLOOD OF CHRIST IS A POWERFUL AGENT OF CONTINUAL CLEANSING

Continual Cleansing

It is important in this scripture that we center on the word *cleanses*. This denotes a continual cleansing process. Though we have been redeemed and are living for Christ, it is important to understand that God has made provision for our continual cleansing.

In John's writing to the early church he said, "My little children, these things I write to you, so that you may not sin. And if anyone sins, we have an Advocate with the Father, Jesus Christ the righteous. And He Himself is the propitiation for our sins, and not for ours only but also for the whole world" (1 John 2:1, 2).

Continual Repentance

These scriptures tell us that the possibility of us sinning after redemption exists. We are not to practice sin. Sin is not to be a lifestyle for us, but if we do sin we need to understand that the blood of Christ has been appropriated to cleanse us from that sin. Therefore, we need to understand that continual repentance to God is a privilege that He gives us because of the shed blood of His Son.

No Condemnation

There is a tendency among some to grow discouraged because of failures, mistakes and sins committed once they have started following Christ. There is a subtle attack that the Enemy uses, and that tactic is condemnation. Satan wants to condemn us. In fact, his title is "the accuser of the brethren." He would continually accuse us before God for our sins and transgressions; however, this passage in 1 John lets us know that there has been a provision made for us to be cleansed, over and over again.

God teaches in His Word that we are not to practice sin as a lifestyle. In fact, Paul was very emphatic when he asked, "What shall we say then? Shall we continue in sin that grace may abound? Certainly not! How shall we who died to sin live any longer in it?" (Romans 6:1, 2).

No Sinful Lifestyle

Paul is saying that a believer can no longer live in a sinful lifestyle. A believer is not to take advantage of the grace of God, for when he takes advantage of the grace of God and falls into a sinful lifestyle of continual sin, he then forfeits the grace of God. Romans 6:23 becomes his future: "For the wages of sin is death, but the gift of God is eternal life in Christ Jesus our Lord." God has made a provision for the believer's continual cleansing as he walks with God and needs the blood appropriated to his life.

Applying the Truth
MY DAILY WALK WITH GOD

If I sin, what should I do? _____

_____

_____

_____

Read and meditate upon the following scriptures concerning abstinence from sin: 1 Thessalonians 5:22; James 4:7; 1 Peter 1:16; 1 John 2:1.

ILLUSTRATION

Shaping for the Highest

During the war years, a faithful minister went through a devastating time. He had lost many of his loved ones, and then his precious wife passed away. His life was devastated and he felt he could no longer go on. In deep discouragement he wondered why God was allowing these things to happen in his life and why he was going through such a dark valley. One day, while walking along the street, he happened to pass a building under construction. He saw that it was a church building and noticed that a stonemason was working on the ground, very carefully chiseling, hammering and shaping a stone. He asked the stonemason what he was doing, and the stonemason gave him an answer that he would never forget. "I am shaping this stone down here so it will fit up there, "he said, pointing to the gable of the building. The minister was able to see that indeed when the stone was properly shaped, it would fit perfectly in the highest place of the building. God spoke to his heart that day and told him how He was continually shaping and cleansing his life so he would fit in the highest place that God could put him. So it is with the blood of Jesus. Daily He cleanses, shapes and molds our lives so we can fit in the highest place that God has for us.

THE BELIEVER CAN PLEAD THE POWER OF THE BLOOD FOR SPECIFIC NEEDS

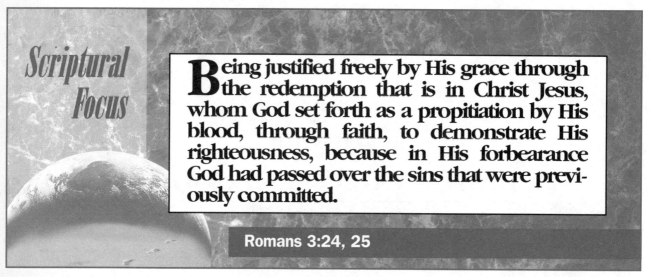

Scriptural Focus

Being justified freely by His grace through the redemption that is in Christ Jesus, whom God set forth as a propitiation by His blood, through faith, to demonstrate His righteousness, because in His forbearance God had passed over the sins that were previously committed.

Romans 3:24, 25

Deliverance From Bondage

We probably do not fully realize how powerful the blood of Christ is to deliver. The greatest deliverance that can occur in any heart is deliverance from the bondage of sin. The bondage of sin is something that we inherit as children of Adam's race, and no other agency can redeem us from that bondage except the blood of Christ. If therefore the blood of Christ is able to break the most powerful of all bondages, certainly the blood of Christ is able to deliver us from any lesser bondage, trial or affliction.

Covering of the Blood

Isaiah 53 graphically illustrates that there are things the blood of Christ was shed for as far as deliverance is concerned. Notice that Isaiah categorically lists the things Christ suffered for. Christ suffered for our griefs and sorrows (v. 4). He was wounded for our transgressions, bruised for our iniquities, His chastisement brings about our peace, and His stripes heal us (v. 5). He bore the sin of many and made intercession for the transgressors, even those who were responsible for His death (v. 12).

The blood of Jesus is able to cleanse and cure us from a multiplicity of ailments, diseases and afflictions. No sickness that ever came to the human race is beyond the scope of the power of Christ to heal. No grief that a mourner has ever borne is beyond the power of the blood of Christ to assuage and comfort. No sorrow that has ever shattered a heart is beyond the power of Christ's blood. Though our sins may be many and great, they still come under the dominion and power of the blood of Christ. Therefore, the believer has the wonderful privilege to call upon and plead the power of the blood to deliver him in his day of trouble.

Applying the Truth
MY DAILY WALK WITH GOD

◆ In the Book of Acts—which tells of the early church after the resurrection of Christ—look up at least five instances where divine healing occurred because the church prayed and believed in the power of the blood of Christ to heal.

◆ Ask a Christian friend to share with you testimonies of divine deliverance that occurred as a result of prayer.

◆ Think of someone you know who is in desperate need of a divine touch from God and spend a few moments today pleading the power of the blood of Christ for his/her divine touch.

SATAN HAS NO POWER TO COUNTERACT THE BLOOD OF CHRIST

Scriptural Focus

Then I heard a loud voice saying in heaven, "Now salvation, and strength, and the kingdom of our God, and the power of His Christ have come, for the accuser of our brethren, who accused them before our God day and night, has been cast down. And they overcame him by the blood of the Lamb and by the word of their testimony, and they did not love their lives to the death.

Revelation 12:10, 11

**Satan Not
Coequal**

Many people have the mistaken idea that Satan—the accuser of the brethren and the enemy of God and His saints—has attributes that are coequal with God. Nothing could be further from the truth. Satan is a created being (Ezekiel 28). His power is limited and certainly is not greater than that of the Creator.

**Blood and
Word**

In Revelation 12, John shares with us the triumph of the saints of the Most High God. It is interesting to note that when Satan, who accused them before God day and night, was defeated, he was overcome by two elements—the blood of the Lamb and the word of the saints' testimony. This tells us immediately that Satan does not have the power to counteract, overcome or undo the work of the power of the blood of Christ. In fact, he is defeated constantly by the power of the shed blood of the Son of God. It is the one thing that he cannot duplicate or counterfeit. The blood of Christ is so precious, so holy and so unique that there is no substitute in the entire universe. Nothing can do what the blood is able to do, and Satan has no power where the blood of Christ is concerned.

Throughout the New Testament, preachers constantly preached about the power of the blood. When Paul preached to the Corinthian church, he declared that he was determined not to know anything among them "except Jesus Christ and Him crucified" (1 Corinthians 2:2). To the Romans, he declared that his message was the message of the gospel of Christ, and because of that message he was a debtor to them (Romans 1:14-16). This mentor of the gospel would tell the young preacher Timothy, his student, that there was no message more worthy of acceptance than the message of Christ and His sacrifice (1 Timothy 1:15).

**Price of
Redemption**

The apostle Peter reminded his readers that only the precious blood of Christ was a high enough price to pay for their redemption (1 Peter 1:19). Throughout the Book of Hebrews, the writer of this powerful epistle emphasized that the blood of bulls and goats and the ashes of heifers were insufficient to cleanse them of their depraved condition. Only the blood of Christ had the ability to change their lives and make them acceptable to God.

**Jews and
Romans**

The New Testament church preached the power of the blood, for Satan fought the church relentlessly in its infancy. Satan's instruments included the Judaizers and the Jewish faith that had risen up against Christianity, but in a more powerful fashion his chief instrument was the throne of Caesar and the power of Rome. Yet history will testify to the fact that Rome was ultimately powerless against the blood of Christ. For though Rome could kill and martyr Christians, they were unable to stop the redeeming power of Christ's blood.

Satan has no power against the blood in the believer's life. He cannot eradicate its effect in the human heart unless that heart turns away from God.

Applying the Truth

MY DAILY WALK WITH GOD

Read Ezekiel 28 and Isaiah 14 to learn of Satan's rise and fall.

Read Matthew 4:1-11 to understand Christ's temptation and victory over the devil.

Why does God require a sacrifice of blood for the remission of sin?

_____

_____

_____

When did God begin to teach the human race about the necessity

of the shedding of blood? _____

_____

_____

What were God's intentions in introducing the Old Testament's

sacrificial system? _____

_____

_____

_____

Why do you think Israel failed to see Christ as Messiah when He

finally came to earth? _____

_____

_____

_____

What did the Passover lamb represent to God's people in the Old

Testament, and how is the Passover lamb a symbol of Christ?

_____

_____

◆ In what passage does the Bible tell us that Christ's blood cleanses us from all unrighteousness? _____

_____

_____

_____

◆ Name the three agents of sanctification in the human heart.

_____

_____

◆ Why must we repent each time we transgress against God? ____

_____

_____

◆ What things other than redemption was the blood of Christ shed for?_____

_____

_____

◆ Why does Satan not have power to counteract the blood of Christ?

_____

_____

_____

LESSON REVIEW

Justification is the theological name for God's action of forgiveness and cleansing that places man in fellowship with God. It is one of the key doctrines of Scripture.

The Old Testament institution and practice of the sacrificial system reflected God's desire to forgive sinful people and man's need for a price to be paid in order for forgiveness to take place. The blood shed by sacrificial animals paid the redemption price. While sacrifices were efficacious for those who offered them, the Mosaic system eventually degenerated into mere form and ritual.

The New Testament makes it clear that the shedding of Christ's blood on the cross was the once-and-for-all payment for man's sin. His blood provides initial redemption and continuing cleansing. He has won a victory over death and hell that assures believers of their final victory.

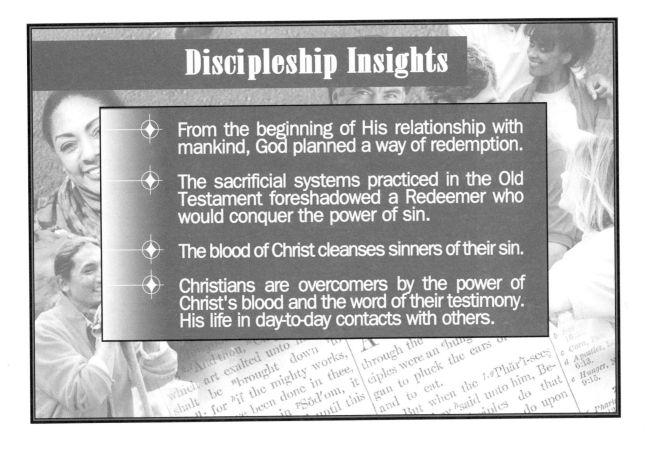

Discipleship Insights

◆ From the beginning of His relationship with mankind, God planned a way of redemption.

◆ The sacrificial systems practiced in the Old Testament foreshadowed a Redeemer who would conquer the power of sin.

◆ The blood of Christ cleanses sinners of their sin.

◆ Christians are overcomers by the power of Christ's blood and the word of their testimony. His life in day-to-day contacts with others.

Resources

Griffis, David M. *Spirit Wars*. Cleveland, TN: Pathway Press, 1994.

Barnhouse, Donald Gray. *The Romans Commentaries*. Grand Rapids, MI: William B. Eerdmans Publishing Co., n.d.

Pentecost, J. Dwight. *Your Adversary the Devil*. N.p.: Zondervan Publishing Co., nd.

Hayford, Jack W. *Hayford's Bible Handbook*. Nashville, TN: Thomas Nelson Publishing Co., n.d.

Sustar, T. David. *Transforming Faith*. Cleveland, TN: Pathway Press, 1992.

Bowdle, Donald. *Redemption Accomplished and Applied.* Cleveland, TN: Pathway Press, n.d.

Conn, Charles W. *Anatomy of Evil.* Cleveland, TN: Pathway Press, 1984.

NOTES:_____

_____

SANCTIFICATION

Living the Sanctified Life

SANCTIFICATIO

6
LESSON

Homer G. Rhea

INTRODUCTION

Separated

Sanctification involves both being separated from sin and separated unto God. Other words used in connection with sanctification, such as *holy* or *perfect*, carry the thought of wholeness, holiness, maturity and completion. Sanctification is a crisis experience subsequent to regeneration and based on faith in the shed blood of Jesus Christ. The work begun in this crisis experience is continued throughout the believer's life. The apostle Paul recognized this when he wrote: "For I am confident of this very thing, that He who began a good work in you will perfect it until the day of Christ Jesus" (Philippians 1:6, *NASB*). This truth is also seen in the apostle Peter's admonition in 2 Peter 3:18: "But grow in the grace and knowledge of our Lord and Savior Jesus Christ."

In speaking of the practical dimension of sanctification, Donald N. Bowdle, in *Redemption Accomplished and Applied*, says the concept includes the following:

- The *formal* cause is the love of God (1 John 4:10)

- The *meritorious* cause is the blood of Jesus Christ (1 John 1:7)

- The *efficient* cause is the Holy Spirit (Titus 3:5; 1 Peter 1:2)

- The *instrumental* cause is truth (i.e., the Word of God, John 17:17)

- The *conditional* cause is faith (Acts 15:9; 26:18).

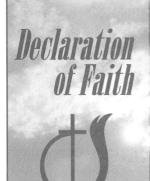

Declaration of Faith

We believe in sanctification subsequent to the new birth, through faith in the blood of Christ; through the Word, and by the Holy Ghost (Romans 5:2; 1 Corinthians 1:30; 1 Thessalonians 4:3; Hebrews 13:12).

Article 6

Scriptural Focus

If we walk in the light as He is in the light, we have fellowship with one another, and the blood of Jesus Christ His Son cleanses us from all sin (1 John 1:7).

Sanctify them by Your truth. Your word is truth (John 17:17).

To [those] . . . elect according to the foreknowledge of God the Father, in sanctification of the Spirit, for obedience and sprinkling of the blood of Jesus Christ (1 Peter 1:1, 2).

1 John 1:7 ✦ John 17:17 ✦ 1 Peter 1:1, 2

THE BLOOD OF JESUS

The blood of Jesus not only provides forgiveness for sins; it provides cleansing as well. John affirmed this when he wrote: "If we confess our sins, He is faithful and just to forgive us our sins and to cleanse us from all unrighteousness" (1 John 1:9).

There is neither forgiveness nor purity apart from faith in Jesus Christ. His blood is both necessary and sufficient to cleanse us from all sin. We are cut off from the favor of God without the cleansing work of the blood of Jesus.

Cleansing From Sin

Offering Without Blemish

Jesus shed His blood voluntarily. He was driven by love for all humanity. Since His life was sinless, His offering of Himself was without blemish. Thus, it was acceptable unto God. His sacrifice was not only human but divine. Its character was not temporary and changeable, but permanent and eternal. The effect of such a sacrifice was cleansing and life. Comparing Christ's sacrifice with that of bulls and goats in the Old Testament, the writer of Hebrews asked: "How much more shall the blood of Christ . . . cleanse your conscience from dead works to serve the living God?" (9:14).

The blood of Jesus removed all barriers between God and believers. The blood made atonement for men's sins; it answered the Law; it removed the curse; it broke down the wall of partition; it provided cleansing for the soul; and it made boldness before God possible. The only way of entrance into God's presence is by the blood of Jesus. And the only way to cleansing and purity is the shed blood of Jesus.

Dearer Than Life

Believers can learn something about the importance of purity from the ermine. In the forests of northern Europe lives the ermine, a small animal best known for his snow-white fur. Instinctively, he protects his glossy coat with great care lest it become soiled. Hunters often capitalize on this trait. Instead of setting a mechanical trap to catch the ermine, they find his home in a cleft of a rock or a hollow tree and daub the entrance and the interior with tar. Then their dogs start the chase, and the frightened ermine flees toward his home. But finding it covered with dirt, he spurns the place of safety. Rather than soil his white fur, he courageously faces the yelping dogs, who hold him at bay until the hunters capture him. To the ermine, purity is dearer than life! (From *Windows on the Word*, Dennis J. DeHaan, compiler, Baker Book House, Grand Rapids, Michigan.)

Applying the Truth
MY DAILY WALK WITH GOD

How important is the redeeming work of Christ to you? _____

_____

_____

_____

What value do you place on inner cleansing and purity of life?

_____

_____

_____

The Word Alive

The Word of God plays an important part in the work of sanctification. The Word is alive. Because it is alive it accomplishes the purpose God has for it. Speaking through Isaiah, God said: "For as the rain and the snow come down from heaven, and do not return there without watering the earth, and making it bear and sprout, and furnishing seed to the sower and bread to the eater; so shall My word be which goes forth from My mouth; it shall not return to Me empty, without accomplishing what I desire, and without succeeding in the matter for which I sent it" (Isaiah 55:10, 11, *NASB*). Jesus prayed, "Sanctify them by Your truth. Your word is truth" (John 17:17).

Searching the Soul

Charles Eerdman wrote that the Word of God searches a man's "inmost desires and motives. It makes evident whether or not he is really seeking for purity and holiness and fellowship with God, or whether lower desires are dominating his soul." He added, "We are responsible to a living God whose all-seeing eye none can escape. He knows perfectly all our disobedience and unbelief, yet He is ready to grant all needed grace as we draw near to Him in the name of Christ."

It is told that many years ago, while on a visit to England, a wealthy businessman was fascinated by a powerful microscope. Looking through its lens to study crystals and the petals of flowers, he was amazed at their beauty and detail. He decided to purchase a microscope and take it back home. He thoroughly enjoyed using it until one day he examined some food he was planning to eat for dinner. Much to his dismay, he discovered that tiny living creatures were crawling in it. Since he was especially fond of this particular food, he wondered what to do. Finally, he concluded that there was only one way out of his dilemma—he would destroy the instrument that caused him to discover the distasteful fact. So he smashed the microscope to pieces!

"How foolish!" you say. But many people do the same thing with the Word of God. They would like to get rid of it because it reveals their evil nature. (From *Illustrations for Biblical Preaching*, edited by Michael P. Green, Baker Book House, Grand Rapids, Michigan.)

Applying the Truth
MY DAILY WALK WITH GOD

Match the scripture with the truth it supports:

The Bible is a light for the path of believers.	1 Timothy 4:5
The Word of God is a sanctifying agent.	John 17:17
The Bible is likened to water for our cleansing.	Psalm 119:105
God's Word is truth.	Ephesians 5:26

Transparent but Strong

In the cathedral of St. Mark in Venice, a marvelous building lustrous with an Oriental splendor beyond description, there are pillars said to have been brought from Solomon's Temple. These pillars are of alabaster, a substance firm and endurable as granite and yet transparent; hence the light glows through them. They are a symbol of what all true pillars of the church should be—firm in their faith and transparent in their character.

Of course, Christians are what they are because of God's love. They are not sanctified because they are good or better than others, but because God has chosen them. Jesus said concerning those who follow Him: "You did not choose Me, but I chose you and appointed you that you should go and bear fruit, and that your fruit should remain, that whatever you ask of the Father in My name He may give you" (John 15:16).

Cooperating With the Spirit

It is the work of the Holy Spirit to sanctify, but the individual cooperates with the Spirit in this exercise. The believer feels the need of being sanctified, is willing to be sanctified, earnestly desires to be sanctified, and yields to the Spirit in His sanctifying work. The Spirit desires to set us apart for God so God can use us in His service. At this point, the believer's life no longer belongs to him to live as he likes; it belongs to God for Him to use as He likes.

Sanctification is obtained through belief of the truth. Faith is action. It is the gift of God, but it is also the act of man. Without God's gift there could be no faith, and without man's exercise of that gift there is no sanctification. Christ and all He offers is received by faith.

Several centuries ago, the emperor of Japan commissioned a Japanese artist to paint a bird. Months passed, then years. Finally, the emperor went to the artist's studio to ask for an explanation. The artist set a blank canvas on the easel and in 15 minutes completed the painting of a bird that became a masterpiece. The emperor asked why there had been such a long delay. The artist then went from cabinet to cabinet; he produced armloads of drawings of feathers, tendons, wings, feet, claws, eyes and beaks of birds; these he placed one by one before the emperor. He was able to produce a masterpiece in a few minutes because he had studied meticulously for years.

Conforming to the Image

The Holy Spirit operates in the life of the believer, so that we may be conformed to the image of God's Son (Romans 8:29). This is not done in the moment of the new birth. That moment is no more than the declaration of the divine purpose; it is just the beginning of the long work. The whole process is a detailed and painstaking progress "until Christ is formed in you" (Galatians 4:19). Then the day shall come when the Emperor of emperors will come for us, and the completed work will flash forth in a moment. "Beloved, now are we the sons of God, and it doth not yet appear what we shall be: but we know that, when he shall appear, we shall be like him; for we shall see him as he is." (1 John 3:2). (From *Let Me Illustrate*, by Donald Grey Barnhouse, Fleming H. Revell Company, Westwood, New Jersey.)

Applying the Truth

MY DAILY WALK WITH GOD

Read John 14—16. Observe the references to the Holy Spirit. List five ways the Spirit relates to believers.

1. _____

2. _____

3. _____

4. _____

5. _____

Answers: (1) He is our Helper (14:16, 26). (2) He will be with us forever (14:16). (3) He is the Spirit of truth (14:17). (4) He is our teacher (14:26). (5) He glorifies Christ (16:14). Note: There are other possible answers.

THE LIFE OF HOLINESS

Matter of the Heart

Sanctification has to do with the heart. As J.I. Packer said in *Rediscovering Holiness*, "Holiness starts inside a person, with a right purpose that seeks to express itself in a right performance. It is a matter, not just of the motions I go through, but of the motives that prompt me to go through them."

Sanctification also has to do with the hands. Genuine sanctification is genuine Christlikeness, and Christlikeness must be lived out on a daily basis. More than a century and a half ago, the Scottish pastor and revival preacher Robert Murray McCheyne declared: "My people's greatest need is my personal holiness."

12 Characteristics

John Charles Ryle lists 12 characteristics of a sanctified person in his book, *Holiness*. These traits provide a checklist for practical sanctification:

1. Holiness is the habit of being of one mind with God, according as we find His mind described in Scripture. It is the habit of . . . hating what He hates, loving what He loves, and measuring everything in this world by the standard of His Word.

2. A holy person will endeavor to shun every known sin, and to keep every known commandment.

3. A holy person will strive to be like our Lord Jesus Christ.

4. A holy person will follow after meekness, long-suffering, gentleness, patience, controlled temper, government of his tongue. He will bear much, forbear much, overlook much, and be slow to talk of standing on his rights.

5. A holy person will follow after temperance and self-denial.

6. A holy person will follow after charity and brotherly kindness.

7. A holy person will follow after a spirit of mercy and benevolence toward others.

8. A holy person will follow after purity of heart.

9. A holy person will follow after the fear of God.

10. A holy person will follow after humility.

11. A holy person will follow after faithfulness in all the duties and relations in life.

12. Last, but not least, a holy person will follow after spiritual-mindedness. To commune with God in prayer, in the Bible, and in the assembly of His people—these things will be the holy person's chief enjoyments.

Applying the Truth

MY DAILY WALK WITH GOD

◆ Reread this section of this study. Reflect upon your own relationship with Jesus Christ. Measure your own experience against the checklist offered by John Charles Ryle.

◆ List ways in which you need to improve in holiness of life._____

_____

_____

_____

CHRISTIAN MATURITY

Maturity in Christ

The goal toward which every believer should be moving is maturity in Christ. The apostle Paul says that God has placed people in the church whose mission is to prepare God's people for works of service, so that the body of Christ may be built up. He sees the whole body growing and building itself up in love, as each part does its work (see Ephesians 4:11-16).

Believers who are moving toward maturity have found their place of service and are doing their part to enhance the cause of Christ. By this gauge they may measure the degree of maturity they have attained.

Rates of Growth

Not everyone arrives at maturity in the same way. Circumstances of life may force some into maturity sooner than others. For example, a lad's father dies and much of the responsibility for the support of the family falls to him. He begins to act in ways that he would not have acted until a few years later, had his father not died. Thus, he is, in a sense, rushed into maturity. But whether one comes to maturity early or later, the results are the same. As a mature person he is ready to give support, rather than crave it or depend upon it. He dares to stand alone if need be—to be an oak, not a vine.

Full-grown

Mature Christians are said to be full-grown men and women. They are grown-up people who act like grown-up people. Paul expressed it this way: "When I was a child, I used to speak as a child, think as a child, reason as a child; when I became a man, I did away with childish things" (1 Corinthians 13:11, *NASB*).

A mature Christian does not look at the obstacles, but rather at God. Donald Grey Barnhouse tells of a dear old woman who had arrived at a mature state in Christ. Someone said to her, "I believe that if you thought the Lord told you to jump through a stone wall, you would jump."

The old lady replied, "If the Lord told me to jump through a wall, it would be my business to jump, and it would be His business to make the hole."

Performing the Promise

It would be impossible to define more simply the exact relationship that maturity brings between the believer and the Lord. Although we do not understand every step of the way by which we must walk, we are fully persuaded that whatever God has promised, He is able to perform (Romans 4:21). We leave all of the matters that are not comprehended to the heart of the God whom we know to be the loving heavenly Father.

Applying the Truth
MY DAILY WALK WITH GOD

> ◆ Spend some time in prayer.
>
> ◆ Seek God's face to help you as you endeavor to take the steps that will lead you to Christian maturity.
>
> ◆ Resolve in prayer that you will be open to all the privileges of a sanctified life.

Since the blood of Jesus Christ provides both forgiveness and cleansing, what is our responsibility if we fail Him (see 1 John 1:9)? _____

_____

_____

A knowledge of the Word of God is essential to a sanctified lifestyle. What systematic plan of Bible study do you have? _____

_____

_____

Different people travel different distances to reach maturity in Christ. Where are you in this ongoing process? _____

_____

_____

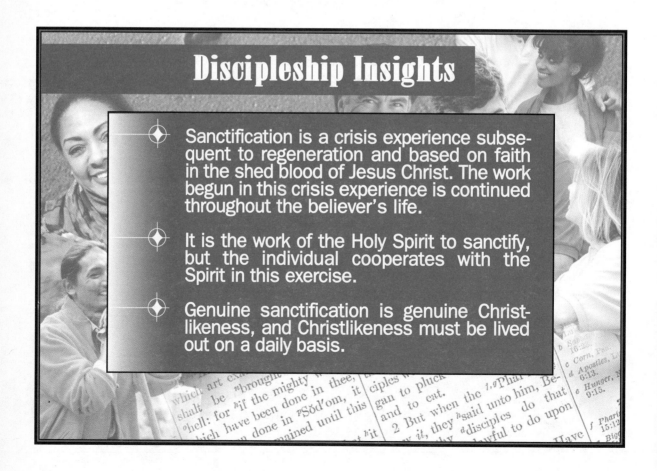

Discipleship Insights

◆ Sanctification is a crisis experience subsequent to regeneration and based on faith in the shed blood of Jesus Christ. The work begun in this crisis experience is continued throughout the believer's life.

◆ It is the work of the Holy Spirit to sanctify, but the individual cooperates with the Spirit in this exercise.

◆ Genuine sanctification is genuine Christlikeness, and Christlikeness must be lived out on a daily basis.

Resources

Bowdle, Donald N. *Redemption Accomplished and Applied*. Cleveland, TN: Pathway Press.

Slay, James L. *This We Believe*. Cleveland, TN: Pathway Press.

Arrington, French L. *Christian Doctrine: A Pentecostal Perspective*, Vol. 2. Cleveland, TN: Pathway Press.

Gause, R. Hollis. *Living in the Spirit*, Cleveland, TN: Pathway Press.

Packer, J.I. *Rediscovering Holiness*. Ann Arbor, MI: Vine Books, Servant Publications.

Five Views on Sanctification, Grand Rapids, MI: Academie Books, Zondervan Publishing House.

NOTES:_____

_____

_____

_____

_____

_____

_____

_____

_____

_____

_____

_____

_____

_____

_____

_____

_____

_____

HOLINESS

Marks of Holiness

7
LESSON

Marcus V. Hand

INTRODUCTION

Called to Be Saints

Disciples are called to be saints and commanded to be holy. But how can one be holy when you take into account both human nature and the kind of world we live in? Can you be holy in the workplace when those around you are unholy and irreverent? Can you participate in recreational activities and maintain the proper standard of purity you should? Is being holy synonymous with being a kook? Is being holy the same as being a nerd? Is the balanced, separated lifestyle that the Bible demands really possible?

World's Goals vs. Christian's Priorities

Widespread cultural rot dominates society and clashes with our sense of decency. The world's media, mores, messages and meanings subtly seduce the soul. Deviancy is treated as the norm. A constant barrage of visual and aural images erode our senses. The "Everybody's doing it, so it must be all right" line is bought by the majority of the people we see. The world's goals, ever at cross-purposes with Christ's causes, conflict with the Christian's priorities.

In this milieu God commands us to be holy, as He is holy; to be perfect, as He is perfect. "Therefore you shall be perfect, just as your Father in heaven is perfect" (Matthew 5:48). Are His demands impractical, if not impossible? What does the Bible and the church say about holiness? Look first at the Scriptural commands.

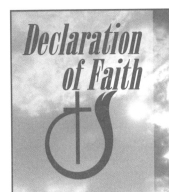

Declaration of Faith

We believe holiness to be God's standard of living for His people (Luke 1:75; 1 Thessalonians 4:7; Hebrews 12:14; 1 Peter 1:15, 16).

Article 7

Scriptural Focus

Pursue peace with all people, and holiness, without which no one will see the Lord: looking carefully lest anyone fall short of the grace of God; lest any root of bitterness springing up cause trouble, and by this many become defiled; lest there be any fornicator or profane person. . . .

Hebrews 12:14-16

THE BIBLE AND HOLINESS

Look up the following Scripture verses:

Leviticus 11:44, 45; 19:2	John 17:19	1 Thessalonians 4:7, 8
2 Timothy 1:9	Hebrews 12:14	1 Peter 1:15, 16

THE CHURCH AND HOLINESS

Church of God teachings on holiness are substantial. The first formal list of church teachings made by the denomination appeared in the August 15, 1910, issue of the *Evening Light and Church of God Evangel*. The sixth item on that list stated simply:

Holiness: Luke 1:75; 1 Thessalonians 4:7; Hebrews 12:14

Holiness Tenets

This basic tenet was reaffirmed at the 1960 General Assembly and again in 1976. (see *Like a Mighty Army*, pp. 137, 138; and *Supplement to the Minutes*, pp. 84, 85.)

Article 7 of the Declaration of Faith states that we believe "holiness to be God's standard of living for His people" (*Supplement to the Minutes*, p. 83).

Practical Commitments

While the term "holiness" is not found in the church's Practical Commitments, this teaching is embodied in every single item of the document. Whether in spiritual matters, moral purity, family responsibility, behavioral temperance, modest appearance, or social obligation, the call to a holiness lifestyle is a fundamental principle woven into the fabric of our beliefs.

The 1960 General Assembly passed a historic "Resolution Relative to Principles of Holiness of Church of God." This resolution was reaffirmed by the General Assembly in 1976 and remains an important part of our core beliefs. It begins:

> The foundation of the Church of God is laid upon the principles of Biblical holiness. Even before the church experienced the outpouring of the Holy Ghost, its roots were set in the holiness revival of the past century. It was, and is, a holiness church—holiness in fact and holiness in name.
>
> The passing of 90 years has not diminished our holiness position or convictions. The years have, instead, strengthened our knowledge that without holiness it is impossible to please God.
>
> We hereby remind ourselves that the Scriptures enjoin us at all times to examine our own hearts. The continuing and consistent life of holiness requires this.

Statement of Vision

Finally, in the Statement of Vision of the Church of God, found in a document called "Scriptural Principles of Ministry," Item 4, declares: "The Church of God is to be a people who hunger for God, experience the presence of God, and stand in awe of His holiness as He changes believers into conformity with Christ."

Church theology and practice call on us to reaffirm our belief and daily practice of Biblical holiness and personal integrity. They remind us to reaffirm our standard of holiness in stated doctrine, in principles of conduct, and as a living reality in our hearts. The motivating rationale is that Christ "has saved us and called us to a holy life—not because of anything we have done but because of his own purpose and grace" (2 Timothy 1:9, *NIV*).

THE DISCIPLE AND HOLINESS

Destined for Better

A Spirit-filled disciple is a decidedly different creature in the world! The moment you believed, the miracle of the new birth occurred in your heart and you became a child of God (see 1 Peter 1:23). Because of this spectacular experience, you are distinctly destined for a better present and a better future.

All believers live on this planet as resident aliens in the world community. In whatever country they reside, Christians are a nation within a nation. Rooted and grounded in eternity, they are separated from unbelievers by the new birth. This distinctive difference is a feeling you probably have already experienced. Even when you think you are most "at home" in the world, you sense a subconscious reality that there is something more. "This world is not my home, I'm just a'passing through!"

Be Holy

God calls His children to holiness: "Be holy as I am holy." This means we must be pure in a wicked world. We must be self-giving in a selfish world. We must love in a dog-eat-dog society. We must show we truly care in a culture that is egocentric and self-serving. Dual dimensions of holiness focus equally on being yielded to God and showing practical, sincere concern for one's neighbor. Holiness fulfills the law of love.

The High Calling

Satan will attempt to sidetrack you from the high calling of practical holiness. Be aware of his divisive ploy. Holiness in heart affects one's language, sex life, demeanor, manners and courtesies, and sensitivities toward others. It affects the books and magazines you read and the videos and television programming you watch. Jesus said, "Blessed are the pure in heart" (Matthew 5:8).

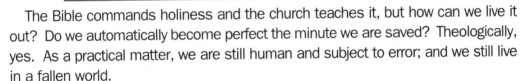

THE PERPLEXING PARADOX

The Struggle

The Bible commands holiness and the church teaches it, but how can we live it out? Do we automatically become perfect the minute we are saved? Theologically, yes. As a practical matter, we are still human and subject to error; and we still live in a fallen world.

For example, no slavery is worse than a sinful habit. Perhaps you struggle with something you know is wrong. You pray for the Lord to help you. You vow never to do it again. You attack the sin. At times you feel you've made progress, then bang! you crash. You wonder if you'll ever attain the holiness you desire.

Another Law

Why this struggle? The Bible says there is "another law at work in the members of my body, waging war against the law of my mind and making me a prisoner of the law of sin" (Romans 7:23, *NIV*). This constant tension entraps and terrifies you. Satan teases, the world lures, the flesh asks, "Why not?"

Old Nature

The old nature doesn't go away. It is a constant, unwelcome companion, ever ready to rise up and sin the second you give it a chance. The key is your response. You respond to your old nature, or you respond to the new. You choose to yield to what God has done in you, or you choose to yield to the flesh. Victory is possible for you because in Christ and through the Holy Spirit you possess a nature you did not have before coming to Christ.

Free to Do Right

Before you came to Christ, you had no choice. Since the Holy Spirit's miracle of new life is in your heart, you are free to do what is right. You may occasionally give in to the old self, but you are not a slave to it. Choosing and doing what is right becomes increasingly easier as you grow in grace. Paul said, "Reckon yourselves to be dead indeed to sin, but alive to God in Christ Jesus" (Romans 6:11).

Look up Ephesians 4:22-24 and discuss with someone what Paul says we have to learn.

Scripture teaches two things about holiness as a practical matter.

HOLINESS IS A GIFT FROM GOD

A Divine Work

Humans struggle to attain holiness through various methods. Religious practice, however, does not make one holy. Nor does isolation or self-flagellation. You can be moral and virtuous. You can climb the tallest tower around and live in it 60 years. You can go live in a cave somewhere or isolate yourself completely from the world. However, none of these give you personal purity. Holiness is a divine work. Only God can make you holy.

Applying the Truth

MY DAILY WALK WITH GOD

Why has God saved us and called us to a holy life (2 Timothy 1:9)?

_____

_____

_____

List 10 kinds of people the Lord Jesus Christ and the Holy Spirit justified and sanctified in 1 Corinthians 6:9-11.

1._____

2._____

3._____

4._____

5._____

6._____

7._____

8._____

9._____

10._____

Match these truths with the appropriate Scripture verse:

Christ has become our righteousness.	Romans 1:17
The righteousness of God is revealed in the gospel.	Matthew 6:33
The Lord is our righteousness.	2 Corinthians 5:21
Seek His righteousness before anything else.	1 Corinthians 1:30
In Christ we become the righteousness of God.	Jeremiah 33:16

HOLINESS IS AN ETHICAL IMPERATIVE

After God has sanctified you and declared you holy, you learn that you are not immune to mistakes or the potential to do wrong. In sanctification, sin does not die to the believer; the believer dies to sin. Herbert Lockyer said, "A person who claims he is so sanctified he cannot sin, actually sins by such an assertion."

Positional holiness is posited in you by God, but there's something you must do to maintain a relational fellowship with Him. Personal, practical holiness must be worked out in daily living. Growing up into the stature of Christ ought to be constantly progressive in experience, but unfortunately you sometimes regress. You find yourself going backward instead of forward.

Ethical Imperative

Working It Out

Applying the Truth
MY DAILY WALK WITH GOD

Read 2 Corinthians 7:1. What is the motivation for "perfecting holiness" in our lives? _____

_____

_____

_____

To do this we must _____

_____ from all

_____ of the _____ and

_____.

Genuine Holiness

You do not become holy by adopting clean habits; only God can make you holy. But you besmirch God's temple, you spoil His holy work in you when you contaminate your body or spirit with unholy practices. James 4:4 warns if we become chummy with the world, we become an enemy of God. Genuine holiness results in striving daily to be like Christ.

Internationally known churchman Dr. R. Lamar Vest wrote: "An increasing number of people seem inclined to seek earnestly for spiritual power but feel no compulsion to link doing wonders for God with living a godly life. Thus we face no greater challenge than that of integrating the language of holiness and power to produce men and women who manifest the signs and wonders of Pentecost while at the same time exemplifying the love and purity of Christ."

Disobedience

It is time for us Christians to face up to our responsibility for holiness. Too often we say we are "defeated" by this or that sin. No, we are not defeated; we are simply disobedient!

It might be well if we stopped using the terms "victory" and "defeat" to describe our progress in holiness. Rather we should use the terms "obedience" and "disobedience." When I say I am defeated by some sin, I am unconsciously slipping out from under my responsibility. I am saying something outside of me has defeated me. But when I say I am disobedient, that places the responsibility for my sin squarely on me.

We may, in fact, be defeated, but the reason we are defeated is that we have chosen to disobey. We have chosen to entertain lustful thoughts, or to harbor resentment, or to shade the truth a little.

Only as we accept our responsibility and appropriate God's provisions will we make any progress in our pursuit of holiness (*The Pursuit of Holiness,* pp. 84, 85).

HALLMARKS OF HOLINESS

A SANCTIFIED MIND

Think Holiness

Talk about holiness too often ignores the mind, as though thinking and belief in holiness are incompatible and contradictory terms. The opposite is true. No one can be completely sanctified unless his mind is sanctified. He cannot live a holy life unless he thinks holy thoughts.

Alienation from God occurs in the mind. Read Colossians 1:21, 22.

Applying the Truth
MY DAILY WALK WITH GOD

According to Romans 12:1, 2 and Ephesians 4:22-24, the transformation of behavior begins with the intellect. Modern psychology agrees with this Biblical principle. Why do you think the principle is true? _____

_____

_____

_____

_____

What does a holy mind think about? (1 Corinthians 13:5; Philippians 4:8) _____

_____

_____

_____

_____

Isaiah 26:3 says that a mind focused on God will be peaceful. Write out Philippians 4:7 in your own words. _____

_____

_____

_____

_____

God includes the intellect when He imputes His righteousness and holiness to a believer. Until a person's mind is changed, any outward holiness is a facade. It is superficial and not genuine. A holy mind is a _____ mind.

SANCTIFIED EMOTIONS

Sanctified Feelings

Another hallmark of holiness in an individual is sanctified emotions. We are, by nature, emotional creatures. Since emotions are the "affective aspect of consciousness," it is safe to say that we are ruled by our emotions. Medical doctors recognize that many sicknesses have their origin in a person's emotional make-up. Most people admit they follow their emotional natures. That is, they do only what they feel like doing.

Never allow your emotions to master you; let God master your emotions! "Above all else, guard your affections. For they influence everything else in your life" (Proverbs 4:23, *TLB*). "A man without self-control is as defenseless as a city with broken-down walls" (25:28, *TLB*).

Passionate for God

The term "sanctified emotions" does not imply that when you become holy, your emotions die. On the contrary, holiness intensifies feelings. The sanctifying Spirit makes one more passionate about life—and God—than ever before. The sanctified person gets angry with the devil, bored with the world, exasperated with the disobedient, excited over witnessing to others, thrilled with salvation, ecstatic over the Holy Spirit baptism, brokenhearted over the lost, and homesick when talking about heaven!

Applying the Truth
MY DAILY WALK WITH GOD

What emotions were displayed in these verses?

Acts 18:25 _____

Romans 12:11 _____

Mark 3:21 _____

Acts 26:24 _____

2 Corinthians 5:13 _____

Read Romans 12:8-12 in *The Living Bible*.

A SANCTIFIED WILL

Sanctified Will

The third hallmark of holiness in a disciple is a sanctified will. The will of man has rightly been called the citadel of the soul. The mind weighs an issue, the emotions bring influence to bear, but it is the will that acts.

Applying the Truth

MY DAILY WALK WITH GOD

What do these verses say about having a weak will (make that "backbone")?

1 Corinthians 15:58 _____

_____

_____

Ephesians 6:14 _____

_____

_____

Ephesians 4:14 _____

_____

_____

James 1:8 _____

_____

_____

What does 1 Samuel 15:23 say about stubbornness? _____

_____

_____

A SANCTIFIED BODY

"I beseech you therefore . . . by the mercies of God, that you present your bodies a living sacrifice, holy, acceptable to God, which is your reasonable service" (Romans 12:1). God expects our bodies to be separated from unclean things and set apart for His exclusive use. "For God did not call us to be impure, but to live a holy life" (1 Thessalonians 4:7, *NIV*).

While only God can make us holy within, the practice of holiness requires a once-and-for-all commitment to live a consecrated lifestyle. Ethical purity is not maintained by accident; it requires deliberate investment in seeking the holiness of God in everything we do and say.

By the very psyche of human nature, in the way God has made us, we want to be holy. We do our best to speak the truth in candor and love. We long to forgive

Holy Bodies

Desire for Holiness

and to be whole people. Holiness is not foreign to our inward yearnings, but it is to the flesh. And the flesh makes us afraid of peer pressure—afraid of what people may think of us. Thus the spirit of this age gradually depresses our living to lower and lower common denominators.

Holiness introduces a new equation in the struggle between our "better yearnings" and the flesh. "Christ, having been raised from the dead, dies no more. Death no longer has dominion over Him. . . . Likewise you also, reckon yourselves to be dead indeed to sin, but alive to God in Christ Jesus our Lord. Therefore, do not let sin reign in your mortal body, that you should obey it in its lusts. And do not present your [body] members as instruments of unrighteousness to sin, but present yourselves to God as being alive from the dead, and your members as instruments of righteousness to God. For sin shall not have dominion over you, for you are not under law but under grace" (Romans 6:9, 11-14).

Daily Holiness

Through His forgiveness and the cleansing power of God, sin is no longer king in our lives. As Jesus sanctified Himself (John 17:19), so we sanctify ourselves daily. "Since we have these promises, dear friends, let us purify ourselves from everything that contaminates body and spirit, perfecting holiness out of reverence for God" (2 Corinthians 7:1, *NIV*).

True holiness is more than a feeling; it is a fruit! (Galatians 5:22, 23). Some suffer under the delusion that when they experience a particular emotion, this means they are holy, they are sanctified. Such people quickly become spiritually depressed when they do not feel this particular emotion.

The Word of God challenges believers to an entire consecration before Almighty God. When the Holy Spirit cleanses the carnal nature, the human will can submit to the divine will in every practical sense. This dynamic reality makes it possible for a holy life to be lived in the home, the school, the workplace and the church.

"To you who believe, He is precious. . . . You are a chosen generation, a royal priesthood, a holy nation, His own special people. . . . Beloved, I beg you as sojourners and pilgrims, abstain from fleshly lusts which war against the soul, having your conduct honorable . . . that when [others] speak against you as evildoers, they may, by your good works which they observe, glorify God" (1 Peter 2:7, 9-12).

LESSON REVIEW

Biblical directives and church theology call on us to reaffirm our belief in, and daily practice of, personal holiness and integrity.

Wherever Christians reside, they comprise a nation within a nation. Rooted and grounded in eternity, believers are separated from unbelievers by the experience of the new birth. Something deep within witnesses to the born-again believer that he or she is not at home in this earth.

We are not inoculated from the pull of the old sin nature, however. Constant tensions arise between the law of Christ and the law of sin and death, which is in the flesh. The believer can resolve the conflict only through a total commitment to Christ and by living daily in the Spirit.

Four hallmarks of a holy life are:

1. A sanctified mind
2. Sanctified emotions
3. A sanctified will
4. A sanctified body

Through redemption's forgiveness and cleansing, our lives can testify to the truth that Jesus Christ, not sin, is king in our lives. This is a life of holiness.

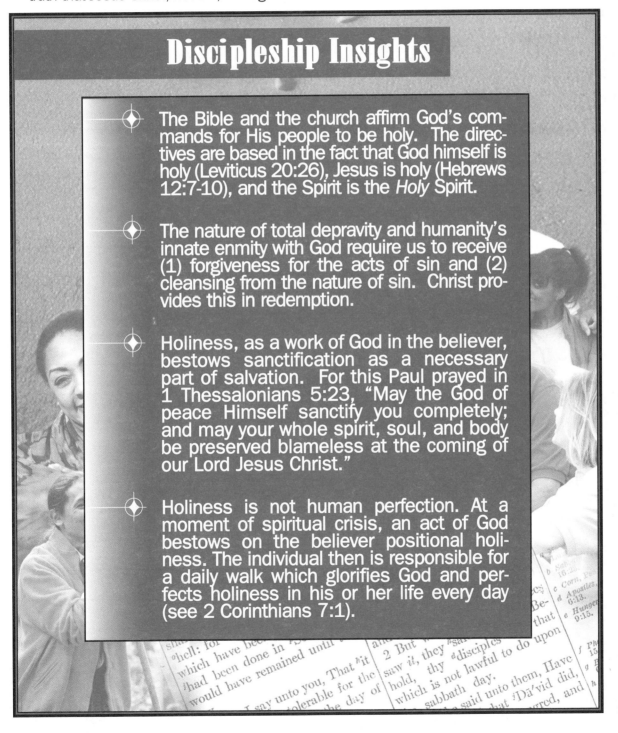

Discipleship Insights

- The Bible and the church affirm God's commands for His people to be holy. The directives are based in the fact that God himself is holy (Leviticus 20:26), Jesus is holy (Hebrews 12:7-10), and the Spirit is the *Holy* Spirit.

- The nature of total depravity and humanity's innate enmity with God require us to receive (1) forgiveness for the acts of sin and (2) cleansing from the nature of sin. Christ provides this in redemption.

- Holiness, as a work of God in the believer, bestows sanctification as a necessary part of salvation. For this Paul prayed in 1 Thessalonians 5:23, "May the God of peace Himself sanctify you completely; and may your whole spirit, soul, and body be preserved blameless at the coming of our Lord Jesus Christ."

- Holiness is not human perfection. At a moment of spiritual crisis, an act of God bestows on the believer positional holiness. The individual then is responsible for a daily walk which glorifies God and perfects holiness in his or her life every day (see 2 Corinthians 7:1).

Resources

Bridges, Jerry. *The Pursuit of Holiness*. Colorado Springs, CO: NavPress Publishing Group, n.d.

Conn, Charles W. *Like a Mighty Army*. Cleveland, TN: Pathway Press, 1996.

Minutes of the 67th General Assembly of the Church of God. Cleveland, TN: Church of God Publishing House, 1996.

Whitney, Donald S. *Spiritual Disciplines for the Christian Life*. Colorado Springs, CO: NavPress Publishing Group, 1991.

NOTES:_____

_____

_____

_____

_____

_____

_____

_____

_____

_____

_____

_____

_____

_____

_____

_____

_____

_____

_____

_____

HOLY SPIRIT

Work of the Holy Spirit in the Life of the Believer

LESSON 8

Ray H. Hughes Sr.

INTRODUCTION

Unknown Person

There is such an appalling lack of knowledge concerning the Holy Spirit and His ministry that He has been referred to as the "Unknown Person of the Godhead."

There are many believers who know of Him but perceive Him to be an influence or energy and not a person. This ignorance arises, in a measure, from the fact that the Holy Spirit does not speak of Himself but of the Father and the Son—for His mission is to glorify Christ.

Who He Is

The apostle Paul met disciples in Ephesus whom he asked, "Did you receive the Holy Spirit when you believed?" Their response was, "We have not so much as heard whether there is a Holy Spirit" (Acts 19:2). The Scripture declares we can know Him and know who He is.

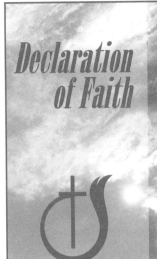

We believe in the baptism with the Holy Ghost subsequent to a clean heart (Matthew 3:11; Luke 24:49, 53; Acts 1:4-8).

We believe in speaking with other tongues as the Spirit gives utterance and that it is the initial evidence of the baptism of the Holy Ghost (John 15:26; Acts 2:4; 10:44-46; 19:1-7).

Article 8 ✦ Article 9

Scriptural Focus

The Spirit of truth, whom the world cannot receive, because it neither seems Him, nor knows Him; but you know Him, for He dwells with you and will be in you.

John 14:17

As He dwells in us and takes full possession of our life, He is revealed to us in His fullness: "It is the Spirit who bears witness, because the Spirit is truth" (1 John 5:6).

Because the Spirit is so little known and recognized in the church, the manifestation of the Spirit is weak. But as the Spirit is recognized, His presence will be self-evidencing. There is no way of knowing the Holy Spirit but through possessing Him and being possessed of Him. To live in the Spirit is to walk in the Spirit. When He is in us, working with us, "both to will and to do for His good pleasure" (Philippians 2:13), the eyes of our understanding are enlightened and we can know Him in the fullness of the blessing of the gospel of Christ.

Self-Evident Presence

◈ He is a person to whom personal characteristics are ascribed and to whom men perform actions.

Personal

◈ He is God the Holy Spirit, the third person of the Trinity, personally distinct from the Father and the Son, occupying a coordinate rank with other members of the Godhead.

◈ He is the administrator of the affairs of the church.

Under these three broad headings, let us look briefly at who the Holy Spirit really is.

More Than Influence

He is as truly a person as is the Father or the Son. As compared with other members of the Godhead, He may seem impersonal. When one views the handiwork of God, the personality of the Father is easier to comprehend. The incarnation of Christ resolves any doubt of His personality for most people. But by some the Holy Spirit is considered a mere influence or a divine energy without personality. He is viewed as mystical or figurative, which tends to discount real personality. The symbols—oil, water, breath, wind and fire—used to describe Him seem to lend credence to the theory that He is merely an influence.

Personality

To deny that He is a person is to deny that He is equal with the Father and with the Son. This is a form of unitarianism that allows for the belief that the Father, Son, and Holy Ghost are in Jesus Christ. Of course, those of us who are Trinitarians deny this position because we believe that the Holy Ghost is a person just as Jesus Christ is a person. The Scripture reveals that the Spirit has a mind, knowledge, a will and emotions, all of which are personal (Romans 8:27; 1 Corinthians 2:10, 11; 12:11; Ephesians 4:30). Therefore, He is more than an abstract quality. He is One in whom intelligence and will reside. He is a person.

Personal Presence

The masculine pronoun applied to Him and the nature of His mission attest to His personality. In the Greek language, the word for *spirit* is a neuter noun and, according to Greek usage, referential pronouns should be neuter; yet, in reference to the Holy Ghost, the masculine pronoun *He* is used, which supports the doctrine of the personality of the Holy Ghost. There are cases, however, in which the natural Greek construction is used; but the amazing fact is that the neuter construction is set aside in favor of the masculine, personal pronoun to give proof of the personality of the Holy Ghost. This change of gender and the use of the masculine, demonstrative pronoun is set forth in John 14:26; 16:13, 14; and elsewhere.

Personal Mission

"But the Comforter, which is the Holy Ghost, whom the Father will send in my name, he shall teach you all things, and bring all things to your remembrance, whatsoever I have said unto you" (John 14:26, KJV). "Howbeit when he, the Spirit of truth, is come, he will guide you into all truth: for he shall not speak of himself; but whatsoever he shall hear, that shall he speak: and he will shew you things to come. He shall glorify me: for he shall receive of mine, and shall shew it unto you" (16:13, 14, KJV). His mission also verifies His personality. When Jesus departed from the earth, He promised to send another Comforter who would take His place. It was not an abstract quality or an influence Christ alluded to. He said He would ask the Father to send another Comforter, the sender being different from the person sent. And certainly He was not speaking of sending an abstract quality or an influence to take the place of the visible Jesus Christ. To deny the personality of the Spirit in this case is to deny the personality of Christ, whose place He came to fill.

Applying the Truth

MY DAILY WALK WITH GOD

According to John 14:17, who is the Holy Ghost? _____

_____

_____

_____

_____

What four attributes indicate that the Holy Ghost is a person and

not a mere influence or force? _____

_____

_____

_____

HE IS GOD THE HOLY GHOST

Coordinate Rank

The third person of the Trinity, personally distinct from the Father and the Son, occupies a coordinate rank with other members of the Godhead.

The deity of the Holy Ghost is clearly established in the Word. He is called the Spirit of God, as Jesus Christ is called the Son of God. He possesses divine attributes. Incommunicable acts of creation and providence are ascribed to Him. The name of God is given to Him in Scripture, and He is given a coordinate rank with the Father and the Son.

Attributes

The divine attributes ascribed to the Spirit are as follows:

Omnipotence: He is all-powerful. The Holy Spirit is all-powerful in that He "searches all things," guides "into all truth," and teaches "all things" (John 14:26; 16:13; 1 Corinthians 2:10, 11).

Omniscience: He is all-knowing. The omniscience of the Spirit is affirmed in 1 Corinthians 2:10: "But God has revealed them to us through His Spirit. For the Spirit searches all things, yes, the deep things of God." He has perfect knowledge of the hidden counsels of God. He knows all things, even the deep things of God, and has the ability and knowledge to search all things.

Omnipresence: He is everywhere. This attribute is vividly described in Psalm 139: "Where can I go from Your Spirit? Or where can I flee from Your presence?" (v. 7). He is omnipresent in essence, and the fact He is everywhere at all times cannot be denied.

Also, the fact that He is eternal is mentioned repeatedly in the Scripture. "And the Spirit of God was hovering over the face of the waters" (Genesis 1:2). "How much more shall the blood of Christ, who through the eternal Spirit offered Himself without spot to God, cleanse your conscience from dead works to serve the living God?" (Hebrews 9:14).

INCOMMUNICABLE ACTS

Acts

The incommunicable acts of creation and providence are set forth in the Scripture through His work in the creation of man and also in the creation of the universe (Genesis 2:7; Job 33:4; Psalm 104:30).

This Holy Ghost is God. He has a divine personality like that of the Father and the Son with whom He is of equal rank. There are Biblical examples where He is called Holy Ghost in one clause and God in another, such as Acts 5:3, 4. Ananias lied to the Holy Ghost: through this act, he had "not lied to men but to God" (v. 4). Thus, the Scripture establishes that the Holy Ghost is God.

COORDINATE RANK

One With the Father

The coordinate rank in which the Holy Spirit is placed with the Father and the Son is expressed often in Scripture. For example, when Jesus was being baptized, the Spirit of God descended upon Him and God spoke from heaven. At the time of the outpouring of Pentecost, Christ was exalted at the right hand of the Father; He entreated the Father for the Holy Ghost, and the Holy Ghost was sent to believers. "Therefore being exalted to the right hand of God, and having received from the Father the promise of the Holy Spirit, He poured out this which you now see and hear." (Acts 2:33).

One With the Son

His coordinate rank is seen again in Ephesians 2:18: By Christ we "have access by one Spirit to the Father." The Holy Spirit's placement in the Godhead is clearly demonstrated through this apostolic benediction: "The grace of the Lord Jesus Christ, and the love of God, and the communion of the Holy Spirit, be with you all" (2 Corinthians 13:14).

HE IS THE ADMINISTRATOR OF THE AFFAIRS OF THE CHURCH

Administrator

The Spirit is the chief administrator of the church. This is beautifully portrayed in Acts 15:28. When the announcement of the decisions of the Council of Jerusalem was made, Peter said, "It seemed good to the Holy Spirit, and to us." Their conclusions were joint conclusions. The Spirit was their fellow counselor. The Spirit of

God sat with them in their deliberations and was their chief adviser. When the decisions were made, the Holy Ghost joined with the apostles and elders by putting His seal of approval upon them. He was assembled with them in business and presided in their deliberations.

Consideration

This should be a lesson for all church councils and councillors. The Holy Spirit will administer the affairs of the church when He is given consideration. When He is recognized, revered and respected as the presiding officer, He actually exercises all of His blessed offices of administration—leading, teaching, guiding and governing the body of Christ. When decisions are reached in this climate, it seems good not only to us but to the Holy Ghost.

Personal Revelation

A believer may have a knowledge of what the Scripture says about the Holy Spirit and yet know little of Him personally. The Word alone cannot teach us to know the Spirit. The Word is the test of our knowledge. The Spirit must be in us. When we know Him, He will reveal Himself and will work through us. If we believe He is a person, then we must treat Him and glorify Him as such.

SUPERNATURAL MANIFESTATIONS

Evidences

The word *manifestation* means "making visible, or that which is shown forth or evidenced." In this particular context, manifestations are the evidences of the gifts of the Spirit.

It may be said that a gift of the Spirit is the Holy Spirit doing a specific service through a believer. The gift that is wrought by the Spirit is an expression of divine ability and not the ability of man. Exercise of a spiritual gift is a direct achievement of the Holy Spirit. It is not the use of individual talents nor is it the anointing of those talents. While the Spirit might and does use one's personal talents to His glory, the manifestation of the Spirit is not a mere augmentation to them.

Spiritual Manifestations

It is a notable fact that it is not the natural talents of individuals that count most in the service of God. It is not the wit, wisdom, skill or human ability; neither is it the means, rank, influence nor personality of a man that determine his effectiveness for God, but it is the manifestation of the Spirit that is bestowed upon him. "But God has chosen the foolish things of the world to put to shame the wise, and God has chosen the weak things of the world to put to shame the things which are mighty; and the base things of the world and the things which are despised God has chosen, and the things which are not, to bring to nothing the things that are, that no flesh should glory in His presence." (1 Corinthians 1:27-29). The excellency of the power is of God and not of us (see 2 Corinthians 4:7). It is the Spirit of God who equips people with the gifts of the Spirit, the exercise of which is under His control, and the means by which the church is enabled to fulfill its mission in the world.

Profiting the Church

Spiritual gifts are bestowed that believers may profit the church. They are not given for show or display but for service, not for self-gratification or self-aggrandizement but for edification, not to exalt or magnify those through whom they are manifested but to strengthen the body of Christ. "The manifestation of the Spirit is given to each one for the profit of all" (1 Corinthians 12:7). "The profit of all" denotes the good of the church. This is the common object of all spiritual gifts. They are not designed mainly for the benefit or gratification of their recipients, but for the good of the church. One writer expressed it in this manner: "Just as the power of vision is not for the benefit of the eye, but for the man."

Gifts for God's Glory

A good test of a true manifestation of the Spirit is that it profits and benefits both the individual concerned and the body of believers to which he ministers. What has been given, regardless of the nature of the gift, is to be used for the edification of the church and not for any selfish purpose. One often sees a distortion of God's purpose through those who would take glory to themselves.

When Simon Magus saw the manifestation of the Spirit in Samaria, he sought to receive this power so as to make a reputation for himself. Whatever we do in word or in deed must all be done to the glory of the Lord (see 1 Corinthians 10:31; Colossians 3:17). The manifestation of the Spirit is threefold: to men, with men, and through men.

Applying the Truth
MY DAILY WALK WITH GOD

Are spiritual gifts natural talents? _____

_____

_____

In what three ways is the manifestation of the Spirit given among men? _____

_____

_____

What was the sin of Simon Magus of Acts 8? _____

_____

_____

◆ How is this seen in the church today? _____

_____

_____

◆ Why is this wrong? _____

_____

_____

THE MANIFESTATION TO MEN

Fire

Scripture gives many examples of the manifestation of the Spirit to men. On the Day of Pentecost the Holy Ghost appeared to men in "cloven tongues like as of fire" (Acts 2:3, KJV). The Spirit arrested the attention of the people and there was a consciousness of God's presence. As a result people were amazed, confounded, convicted, convinced and converted.

Dove

The Holy Spirit is preeminently the Spirit of love and grace. At times in the Scripture He is manifested as a dove, because the dove is the most affectionate of all birds.

Judgment

But because God demands truth in the inward parts, He is also manifested as the Spirit of truth and He guides men into all truth. Although He is the Spirit of love and grace, He also manifests Himself to men through acts of judgment. When Ananias and Sapphira lied to the Holy Spirit, they were both struck dead instantly. He expressed and exhibited in one startling example His abhorrence for those who lie to the Holy Spirit.

Throughout history there are records of the judgment of the Spirit upon people and congregations who have sinned against Him. As a result of His judgment, "great fear came upon all the church and upon all who heard these things" (Acts 5:11), that they may know that He rules in the kingdom of men.

THE MANIFESTATION WITH MEN

Miracles

The Holy Spirit works with men to confirm the Word. Signs, wonders and miracles accompany their ministry to confirm their testimony. "And they went out and preached everywhere, the Lord working with them and confirming the word through the accompanying signs" (Mark 16:20). These signs were a confirmation of the grace and power of the messenger and an evidence of his connection with divine power. They were seals of God's approval upon the ministry. They were legitimizing acts to substantiate their claim as messengers from God. The apostle Paul speaks of himself as having the "signs of an apostle" (2 Corinthians 12:12). "God also bearing witness both with signs and wonders, with various miracles, and gifts of the Holy Spirit, according to His own will" (Hebrews 2:4). The apostle Peter, on the Day of Pentecost, indicated that the signs, wonders and miracles done by the Lord Jesus Christ were a token of approval from God (see Acts 2:22).

Witness

It is a humbling experience for Spirit-filled believers to realize that there is a co-witness of the Spirit. Those who bear witness to the risen Lord Jesus Christ shall find evidence of the Spirit adding His testimony to theirs. He attests to the witness of His people. When the Holy Ghost works with men, He does the miraculous. The Spirit-filled councilmen who were chosen for the ministry of temporalities in the church at Jerusalem were found doing uncommon feats, working signs and wonders among the people, dispensing not only food and clothing, but spiritual graces as well, because the Lord was working with them.

Boldness

The disciples requested that they might be granted boldness for witness through signs of healing (Acts 4:29, 30). They were aware that they could not speak boldly if God did not work mightily. For in the mighty working of His power is the confirmation of our witness.

Power

When Paul and Barnabas had completed their first missionary tour, they returned to Antioch. "Now when they had come and gathered the church together, they reported all that God had done with them, and that He had opened the door of faith to the Gentiles" (Acts 14:27). Likewise, at Jerusalem, "they reported all things that God had done with them" (15:4). They were constantly conscious of the manifestation of the Spirit in their ministry. As a result they kept themselves out of sight. They talked about all that God had done with them, how He had opened the door of faith, and what miracles and wonders God had wrought by them. Nothing is quite so humbling as when we realize our need for reliance upon the Spirit and that His power will cease to be manifested the moment we become self-reliant or self-confident. Our strength is found in the perpetual indwelling and inworking of His Spirit. His presence and presidency must be recognized by us at all times, because He is the official head of all of our affairs.

THE MANIFESTATION THROUGH MEN

Power Through Men

We receive the Holy Spirit as Christ's ascension gift, then we commit ourselves to His indwelling, inworking and outworking. We receive Him by opening our heart to His fullness, then we give Him full possession and power, service and control of our entire being. This includes every faculty of our mind, every affection of our heart, and complete obedience to His bidding. His will becomes ours, and we become servants under His authority. All of His power is at our disposal, provided we are at His disposal. Our relationship to Him is that of a conductor of electricity. The power resident in the source is transmitted through us. It does not belong to us. It is not ours. Power belongs to God, but He manifests Himself through us. With this supernatural power, there is ability for supernatural results.

World evangelization is made possible through the manifestation of the Spirit, because the Spirit has a preeminent place in all true evangelism. It is He who convicts of sin and magnifies Christ. It is through Him and His sovereign work that His gifts are manifested. The confirmation of the Word with signs following is another vital part of God's plan for world evangelization. In fact, God uses signs, wonders and miracles to spearhead His attack against the devil and to convince men of His righteousness.

Applying the Truth
MY DAILY WALK WITH GOD

Why would the manifestation of the Spirit be dependent on our knowledge of Him? _____

_____

Why can't the Word alone teach us everything about the Spirit?

_____

_____

How then are we to use the Word? _____

_____

_____

What is the importance of signs, wonders and miracles? _____

_____

_____

LESSON REVIEW

The Holy Spirit, the third person of the Trinity, should always be referred to as

"He," never "It." He is God, He is personal and He is the administrator of the church.

The Holy Spirit possesses attributes of divinity.

He also manifests His presence in various ways as evidence of the gifts He has given to the church.

Although the limitations of this lesson do no permit a thorough discussion of speaking in tongues, the New Testament pattern of persons being filled with the Holy Spirit reveals that speaking in tongues marked His coming (see Acts 2, 8, 9 10, 11 and 19).

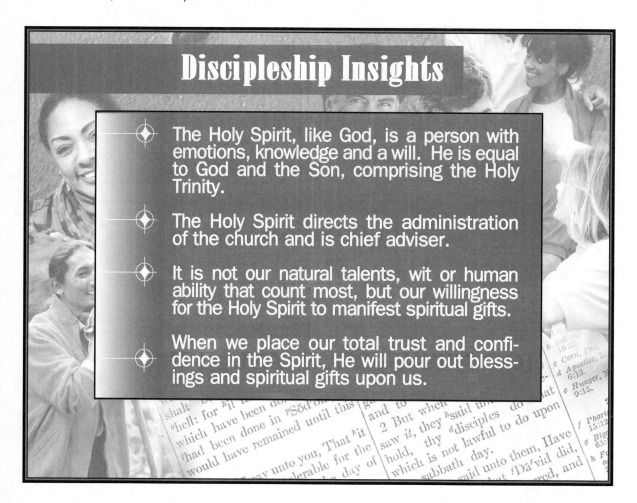

Discipleship Insights

◆ The Holy Spirit, like God, is a person with emotions, knowledge and a will. He is equal to God and the Son, comprising the Holy Trinity.

◆ The Holy Spirit directs the administration of the church and is chief adviser.

◆ It is not our natural talents, wit or human ability that count most, but our willingness for the Holy Spirit to manifest spiritual gifts.

◆ When we place our total trust and confidence in the Spirit, He will pour out blessings and spiritual gifts upon us.

Resources

Arrington, French L. *Christian Doctrine: A Pentecostal Perspective*, Vol. 3. Cleveland, TN: Pathway Press, 1994.

Horton, Stanley. *What the Bible Teaches About the Holy Spirit*. Springfield, MO: Gospel Publishing House, 1978.

Horton, Wade H., ed. *The Glossolalia Phenomenon*. Cleveland, TN: Pathway Press, 1966.

Hughes Sr., Ray H. *Who Is the Holy Ghost?* Cleveland, TN: Pathway Press, 1992.

NOTES:

SACRAMENTS

Necessity of the Sacraments

Daniel F. Boling

9
LESSON

INTRODUCTION

Sacraments

Sacrament is one of those church words which most people do not understand. This results in most churchgoers dropping it from their vocabulary. That is unfortunate, for it is a great word with a great meaning. Webster's dictionary explains it as a religious practice that is considered especially sacred and distinguished from other Christian rites as having been instituted, observed or recognized by Jesus Christ.

The Church of God recognizes three religious practices as being worthy of the name *sacraments*. They are water baptism, the Lord's Supper and footwashing.

Questions

The question before us is, Are water baptism, the Lord's Supper and footwashing essential for proper development as a disciple of Christ? Many people say, "Yes!" Others say, "No!" What does Jesus say? Where does He stand and what did He teach about each of these sacraments? Does He expect His disciples to be active participants in each of these sacraments? If so, should it be a onetime participation, or should disciples participate on a regular basis? Does a disciple have the right to pick and choose which sacraments to follow? What do the Scriptures teach? Let's answer these questions together.

Declaration of Faith

We believe in water baptism by immersion, and all who repent should be baptized in the name of the Father, and of the Son, and of the Holy Ghost. (Matthew 28:19; Mark 1:9, 10; John 3:22, 23; Acts 8:36, 38)

We believe in the Lord's Supper and washing of the saints' feet. (Luke 22:17-20; 1 Corinthians 11:23-26; John 13:4-17; 1 Timothy 5:9, 10)

Article 10 ✦ Article 12

Scriptural Focus

Go therefore and make disciples of all the nations, baptizing them in the name of the Father and of the Son and of the Holy Spirit (Matthew 28:19).

Then He took the cup, and gave thanks, and said, "Take this and divide it among yourselves; for I say to you, I will not drink of the fruit of the vine until the kingdom of God comes." And He took bread, gave thanks and broke it, and gave it to them, saying, "This is My body which is given for you; do this in remembrance of Me." Likewise He also took the cup after supper, saying, "This cup is the new covenant in My blood, which is shed for you (Luke 22:17-20).

"You call me Teacher and Lord, and you say well, for so I am. If I then, your Lord and Teacher, have washed your feet, you also ought to wash one another's feet. For I have given you an example, that you should do as I have done to you" (John 13:13-15).

Matthew 28:19 ✦ Luke 22:17-20 ✦ John 13:13-15

Obedience

After becoming a member of the body of Christ, through faith in Jesus' atoning act of sacrifice, a believer's overwhelming desire is to be and to do everything God wants. To be completely obedient to the Lord of his life, a believer follows the Scriptural directive to be baptized in water. This is revealed in Matthew 28:19; Mark 1:9, 10; John 3:22, 23; and Acts 8:36, 38. Take a few minutes and read each of the scriptures.

Water baptism in the New Testament began with the ministry of John the Baptist. He preached that you must repent of your sins and, following repentance, you must be baptized in water.

Example

Matthew 3:13-17 reveals that Jesus also came to John to be baptized. He did not come because of sin in His life. He came to acknowledge that John's ministry was genuine. He came to identify with John's ministry and to be an example to all believers that baptism was necessary to fulfill all righteousness.

After this baptismal experience, Jesus' disciples performed water baptisms following the conversion of sinners. Before returning to His Father, Jesus commanded His followers to baptize all believers "in the name of the Father, and of the Son, and of the Holy Ghost." There are numerous examples of this practice throughout the Book of Acts, such as the 3,000 responding to Peter's sermon (2:41); the Samaritans (8:12); the Ethiopian eunuch (8:36-38); Paul (9:18); Cornelius and his household (10:47, 48); Lydia (16:14, 15); the Philippian jailer and his household (16:33); Crispus (18:8); and the disciples in Ephesus (19:5).

Testimony

Why is water baptism so important? Primarily it is a testimony of the believer to the world that something significant has happened in his life. That significance is a complete cleansing from sin.

Symbolism

Water baptism is also a sign of entering into the death, burial and resurrection of Jesus (Romans 6:3-5). This is accomplished by being symbolically buried beneath the water and then resurrected unto eternal life when raised up out of the water. This act also signifies that you have been incorporated into the body of Christ and that the church has placed its seal of acceptance upon your relationship with Christ.

Immersion

The Scriptures indicate that the mode of water baptism should be immersion rather than sprinkling of water. The Greek word that is used for "baptism" means to "to dip" or "plunge." Thus, immersion is the method used to fulfill the meaning of Scripture.

Trinitarian

What is the correct "formula" for water baptism? Some insist that you must be baptized only "in the name of Jesus." The apparent motive for this position is to place an emphasis on the oneness of God which would exclude a Trinitarian understanding of God. The reason the Church of God follows the Trinitarian formula is that Jesus commanded it in Matthew 28:19. Also, as Professor Chris Thomas of the Church of God Theological Seminary states, "[It] places a special emphasis on the worship of God in His fullness as Father, Son, and Holy Spirit" (*Ministry and Theology*, p. 167).

When a believer has a good understanding of the spiritual and theological significance of water baptism, it is not necessary to repeat the act. It should be a onetime event. The only reason one should repeat his water baptism is if he reverts to open sin and then returns to Christ after seeking and finding forgiveness for sins. An individual may repeat his baptism if he has some misgivings regarding the original formula or the state of his spiritual condition at the time.

Believers in Christ find water baptism to be one of the major milestones of their relationship with the Master. To follow His example and to be obedient to His Word is one of the most satisfying and fulfilling experiences in the Christian walk. The joy and sense of the Holy Spirit's presence at this sacrament is "joy unspeakable and full of glory."

Onetime

Satisfying

Applying the Truth
MY DAILY WALK WITH GOD

Those who accept Jesus the Messiah as their personal Savior should be baptized in water.

What scriptures verify this statement? _____

_____

_____

Which of these scriptures spoke to you and convinced you that

you should be baptized? _____

_____

_____

Should you repeat your baptism? _____ Why? _____

_____

_____

Why not? _____

_____

What should you do to encourage new believers to be baptized?

_____

_____

Communion

The sacrament of the Lord's Supper is also known as Communion. The institution of this practice is described in Matthew 26:26-29; Mark 14:22-25; Luke 22:15-20; and 1 Corinthians 11:23-26. Before proceeding, take a few minutes and read each of these passages of Scripture.

Passover

On the night before His death by crucifixion, Jesus assumed the position as head of a household and ate the Passover meal with His disciples in Jerusalem. At this meal He gave new and special significance to the bread and wine. After breaking the bread, He distributed it to the disciples and told them it was symbolic of His body which was about to be given for them as well as all other believers. Later in the meal, He passed to them the third cup of the four cups of the meal. He explained to the disciples about the symbolism of this wine: "This is My blood of the new covenant, which is shed for many for the remission of sins" (Matthew 26:28). At the conclusion of the meal Jesus refused to drink from the fourth cup, saying He would not drink again of the fruit of the vine until He drank it anew in the kingdom of God.

Sacrifice

Through this process, Jesus was explaining that the cup of red wine represented His blood which was freely shed to establish a new covenant between God and the world. He willingly offered Himself as a sacrifice for sin in order to bring about a new relationship between God and the redeemed community of believers. Jesus was also pointing toward the full realization of the kingdom of God at the end of the age. When that comes into being, the meal will be resumed at the Marriage Supper of the Lamb.

Remembrance

The Lord instructed His disciples to continue this practice with the bread and the wine. By doing this, the Lord's Supper is eaten in remembrance of His death. Believers also remember that His death brings redemption and reconciliation to God. In addition to the remembrance, the believer expresses a faith in and expectation of the arrival of the kingdom of God in all its fullness.

The observance of the Lord's Supper became a regular part of worship after the coming of the Spirit on the Day of Pentecost (Acts 20:7). Not only was it an act of worship and obedience, but it was a continuation of a rich tradition of fellowship which had been established by Jesus.

The apostle Paul, in 1 Corinthians 11:17-34, has a great deal to say about the process of proper participation in the Lord's Supper. A number of things should be learned as it relates to the practice of this sacrament.

Unity

First of all, the Lord's Supper is a sign of communion between the Lord and His church. It is also to symbolize the communion of the believer with his Lord as well as his communion with other believers. If anything is hindering a believer's relationship with God or someone in the church, this must be corrected before participating in the sacrament. Paul specifically indicated that there were to be no divisions in the body.

Paul also gave a stern warning to believers regarding self-evaluation. Participants are not to "eat this bread, and drink this cup of the Lord, unworthily" (1 Corinthians 11:27, KJV). Many believers convince themselves that they are not worthy of partaking of the Lord's Supper. The enemy of your soul would be pleased if he could persuade you not to participate. However, you must understand what Paul is saying to the Corinthians and to you.

No human is actually worthy enough to be involved in Communion. However, note carefully what Paul has stated. Rather than speaking of the quality of the individual, he is speaking of the manner of participation.

Worthy

"Unworthily" is an adverb. Adverbs tell how, when, where or why something is done. Paul is actually saying that a person is placing himself in spiritual danger when he participates in the Lord's Supper in a flippant, silly or sacrilegious manner. If your spiritual condition is right with God, you have been made worthy to participate by the sacrifice of Jesus.

It should also be noted that although the Corinthians had spiritual problems which needed to be addressed, Paul never told them not to be involved in this sacrament. Instead, he said to examine yourself, fix the problem if one exists, and "eat of the bread and drink of the cup" (v. 28).

Examine

Believers should participate in this sacrament as often as the opportunity presents itself. Paul stated, "For as often as you eat this bread and drink this cup, you proclaim the Lord's death till He comes" (v. 26). The Lord's Supper is an anticipation of the messianic meal that will one day be shared with Jesus in heaven. Regular and consistent involvement in this sacrament is an outstanding testimony of a believer's faith in what Christ has done, is doing and will do in his life.

Anticipation

Applying the Truth
MY DAILY WALK WITH GOD

Take a few moments and "examine yourself." Can you ever remember a time in your relationship with God when you felt closer to Him than you do at this moment? If you answered "Yes," you have started the process of going away from God. Fix the problem now as you pray, "Search me, O Lord."

Read Matthew 26:26-29, Mark 14:22-25; Luke 22:15-20; and 1 Corinthians 11:23-26, and respond to these questions:

What Jewish feast was Jesus participating in when He instituted the Lord's Supper? _____

_____

What is the believer commanded to do after eating the bread and drinking the cup? _____

_____

What faith statement is a believer proclaiming when he participates in the Lord's Supper? _____

_____

FOOTWASHING

There are two passages of Scripture in the New Testament which support the practice of footwashing. These two texts are John 13:1-20 and 1 Timothy 5:10.

Instituted by Jesus

Despite these Scriptural references to footwashing, a number of denominations do not recognize it as a sacrament. However, there are several churches that do acknowledge it because it was instituted by Jesus. The Church of God accepts it as a sacrament for this reason.

As you study John 13:1-20, you will see that Jesus initiated this practice a short time before His betrayal and death. During the Passover meal, He laid aside His garments, girded Himself with a towel, poured water into a basin, and washed the feet of His disciples. Upon completion of this act, He put His garments back on and again reclined with His disciples. Following a brief discussion and explanation, He commanded His disciples to wash each other's feet.

Participation

Many believers attempt to avoid this sacrament. If they understood its significance, there would probably be a greater degree of participation. You should understand that all believers should participate. It is not optional. There are two reasons for these statements. First of all, you should follow the example of Jesus. He was the leader and Lord of the disciples. Nevertheless, He voluntarily lowered Himself to perform the menial act of washing the feet of His followers. This was simply not done by someone in His position of authority. This was an example that all believers should strive to emulate. Second, Jesus commanded His followers to continue the practice. As a believer and follower of Christ, this command is given specifically to you.

Follow Instructions

Now, look closely John 13:14, 15, 17. In verse 14, the Greek word used for "ought" really implies a sense of obligation. Thus, participation is not just a good idea. As a believer, you are obligated to participate. In verse 15, the Greek word for "example" implies that you are to repeat the illustration or picture you have just received. Jesus was expecting His disciples to do exactly as He had done. In verse 17, Jesus pronounces a blessing on those who know about these things and do them.

Being obedient to the command of Jesus, following His example, and being blessed because of obedience are all valid reasons for participating in footwashing. It should also be noted that when a believer has a deeper understanding of the things of God, it is one of the most gratifying experiences of the believer's relationship with the Lord.

Verse 10 helps the Christian to gain an understanding of the significance of this sacrament. When an individual in the ancient world was invited to a banquet, he would be certain to bathe at home. When he arrived at the house of the host, water would be made available to wash the feet of the guest for the purpose of removing the dust that he had encountered on his journey to the banquet. It was not necessary for the guest to bathe again, but it was necessary to cleanse his feet by removing the accumulated dust.

What is the real meaning of this activity? Professor Chris Thomas gives the answer: "Jesus has taken the analogy of the ancient banquet and turned it into a religious practice. In this sense the one who has bathed is the one who has been baptized. Such a one has no need of rebaptism but only the footwashing. The footwashing, then, is a sign of the continual cleansing available to the believer. In that sense it functions as an extension of baptism—just as baptism was the sign of complete cleansing, footwashing is the sign of continual cleansing" (*Ministry and Theology,* p. 171). Since footwashing is a sign of the forgiveness of sin, it is essential for the growth of the spiritual lives of believers. It helps you maintain a right relationship with God and with your brothers and sisters in the faith.

Applying the Truth
MY DAILY WALK WITH GOD

True or False ___	Footwashing is a sign of complete cleansing.
True or False ___	In footwashing, the issue of humble service is clearly present, but it is secondary to the theme of cleansing.
True or False ___	Jesus commanded His followers to participate in footwashing.
True or False ___	1 Timothy 5:10 does not support the practice of footwashing.

Three Sacraments

The Church of God supports the position that there are three sacraments, which should be followed by all believers. These sacraments are water baptism, the Lord's Supper and footwashing.

Each sacrament was either instituted, observed or recognized by Jesus Christ. He instructed His followers to follow His example by continuing to participate in these sacred Christian rites.

A believer's Christian experience will not be fully satisfying until he follows the Lord's command to participate in each sacrament. It is essential that all Christians are baptized in water and partake regularly of the Lord's Supper and footwashing.

It is much like a weaver following a pattern. Certain colors are placed in a tapestry at the precise directions of the pattern to form the desired design.

By following the pattern of Jesus' life, your life will reach the desired design. Participation in the sacraments will add the right color at the right time to make your life exactly what the Master Weaver wants it to become.

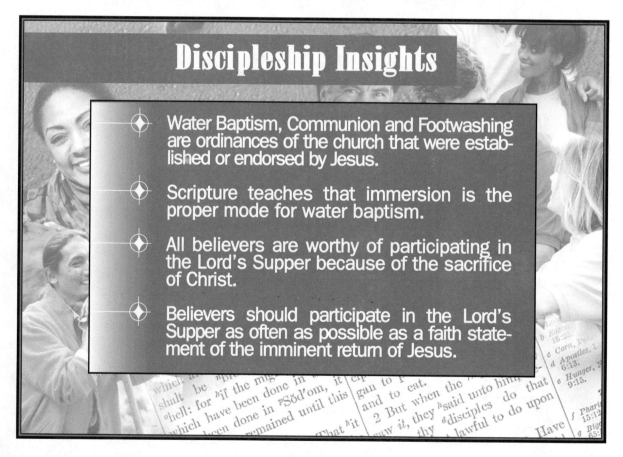

Discipleship Insights

◆ Water Baptism, Communion and Footwashing are ordinances of the church that were established or endorsed by Jesus.

◆ Scripture teaches that immersion is the proper mode for water baptism.

◆ All believers are worthy of participating in the Lord's Supper because of the sacrifice of Christ.

◆ Believers should participate in the Lord's Supper as often as possible as a faith statement of the imminent return of Jesus.

Resources

Barth, Karl. *The Teaching of the Church Regarding Baptism*. London: SCM Press, 1948.

Bromiley, G.W. *Children of Promise*. Grand Rapids: W.B. Eerdmans, 1979.

Cullmann, O. *Early Christian Worship*. Bristol, IN: Wyndham Hall Press, 1953.

Douglas, J.D. and Merrill C. Tenney. *The New International Dictionary of the Bible*. Grand Rapids: Zondervan Publishing Co., 1987.

Higgins, A.J.B. *The Lord's Supper in the New Testament*. Chicago: H. Regnery, 1952.

Thomas, J. Christopher. *Ministry and Theology*. Cleveland, TN: Pathway Press, 1996

NOTES:

_____

_____

_____

_____

_____

_____

_____

_____

_____

_____

_____

_____

_____

_____

_____

_____

_____

_____

_____

HEALING

A Divine Gift and Ministry

10
LESSON

Esdras Betancourt

INTRODUCTION

In Christian theology, the Atonement is the central doctrine of our faith and can properly include all that our Lord accomplished for us through His death as the Lamb of God on the altar of Calvary. Part of that legacy is divine healing. Divine healing is a gift of grace that includes physical, spiritual and emotional (inner-healing) wholeness.

Declaration of Faith

We believe in divine healing is provided for all in the Atonement (Exodus 15:25, 26; Psalm 103:3; Isaiah 53:4, 5; Matthew 8:17; Acts 3:1-26; James 5:14-16; 1 Peter 2:24).

Article 11

DIVINE HEALING IS A SCRIPTURAL MINISTRY

SCRIPTURAL HEALING IN THE OLD TESTAMENT

Both the Old and New Testaments give much attention to bodily health and its relation to spiritual faith. Healing means to make sound or whole. One of the Old Testament words for *health* is *shalom* (peace), which is very inclusive and denotes both physical and spiritual well-being or total wholeness.

In the New Testament the Greek word *astheneo* is translated as "sick" (James 5:14). This word has many meanings, and the context has to be used for its particular meaning.

Astheneo implies different meanings: sickness, physical weakness, character weakness, weakness in faith, human frailty, weakness of understanding, weakness through adversity.

In the Old Testament the basic point is made that God is the healer of His people: "There He made a statute and an ordinance for them. And there He tested them, and said, 'If you diligently heed the voice of the Lord your God and do what is right in His sight, give ear to His commandments and keep all His statutes, I will put none of the diseases on you which I have brought on the Egyptians. For I am the Lord who heals you'" (Exodus 15:25, 26; see also Deuteronomy 32:39). One of God's names is *Jehovah-Rapha*, "the Lord who heals you." The passage may also be rendered, "I am the Lord your physician." This word in Scripture usage is applied to the soul as well as to the body and implies the forgiveness of sins. In Hebrew it conveys the idea, "I will permit none of these diseases upon you, which I permitted upon the Egyptians."

Shalom

God, the Healer

133

First Healing

The first recorded act of healing in the Bible was done through Abraham: "So Abraham prayed to God; and God healed Abimelech, his wife, and his female servants. Then they bore children" (Genesis 20:17).

This concept of healing is echoed also in the Old Testament by the psalmist: "Who forgives all your iniquities, who heals all your diseases" (Psalms 103:3; see also 6:2; 41:4). It is also proclaimed by the prophets (Isaiah 19:22; 53:5; Jeremiah 17:14; Hosea 7:1).

Redemptive Plan

Isaiah 53:4, 5 is also of special interest to us because it shows that healing is part of God's redemptive plan. "Surely he took up our infirmities and carried our sorrows. . . . But he was pierced for our transgressions, he was crushed for our iniquities . . . and by his wounds we are healed" (*NIV*). This takes us back to Genesis 3:15: "And I will put enmity between you and the woman, and between your offspring and hers; he will crush your head, and you will strike his heel" (*NIV*). This presents Christ as the suffering servant and the conquering Savior. Jesus' sufferings had a twofold effect: they were the penalty for sins, and they were the means of reconciliation and restoration. One Hebrew Bible translation, authorized for use by Orthodox Jews, reads: "Our diseases [infirmities] did He bear Himself, and our pains [sorrows] He carried." The wounds (stripes, bruises) are for our healing. Sin is the most devastating disease there is. It kills spiritually and physically.

SCRIPTURAL HEALING IN THE NEW TESTAMENT

The New Testament significantly emphasizes Jesus as the Healer. Mark portrays Him as a teacher and healer in his opening account of Jesus' ministry in Capernaum, with the healing of the demoniac, Peter's mother-in-law, the sick brought to Him in the evening, and the leper (Mark 1:21-45).

Jesus Heals

Jesus healed all who came to Him (Matthew 12:15; 14:36; Luke 4:18, 40; 6:19). Jesus' agenda was this: "The Spirit of the Lord is upon Me, because He has anointed Me to preach the gospel to the poor; He has sent Me to heal the brokenhearted, to proclaim liberty to the captives and recovery of sight to the blind, to set at liberty those who are oppressed" (Luke 4:18). His agenda includes physical and emotional healing. Following Jesus' declaration in the same chapter we read: "All those who had any that were sick with various diseases brought them to Him; and He laid His hands on every one of them and healed them. And demons also came out of many, crying out and saying, "You are the Christ, the Son of God!'" (4:40, 41).

No Conditions

The Gospels clearly show that Jesus' ministry of healing was frequent, complete and abundant. No conditions were imposed. They came by faith—which is equally available to all—and He "healed them all." In meeting physical needs, our Lord healed by a word, by a touch, and by physical anointing. He healed near at hand and at a distance. He healed individuals as well as large groups.

Jesus also commissioned the 12 disciples to proclaim repentance, to cast out demons and to heal the sick (Matthew 10:1; Mark 3:15; 6:13; Luke 9:1, 2, 6). Afterward He sent out 70 with the instruction to "heal the sick" (Luke 10:1-12). The record of Jesus' final commission to His disciples is set forth in Mark 16:15-18: "Go into all the world. . . . He who believes . . . will be saved . . . and [those who are saved] will lay hands on the sick, and they will recover."

Disciples Heal

The Book of Acts tells of the continuation of Jesus' ministry through the Spirit at work in His disciples. This is demonstrated first by the healing of the lame beggar in Jerusalem in the name of Jesus. The healing is clearly intended to point to, and glorify, the person of Jesus and to lead others to faith in Him (Acts 3:1-26). Healing is not an end in itself. It is a means to proclaim the good news of Christ and of the ministry of the Holy Spirit. The Book of Acts records nine examples of individuals healed by the disciples and refers to multiple healings on seven occasions.

Compassion

Why did Jesus heal? The Gospels record 20 cases of individual healings performed by Christ and 10 cases of multiple healings. Those healings expressed not only His compassion for the suffering but also constituted a revelation of His person. This is brought out by the statement of Jesus after healing the paralytic—"that you may know that the Son of Man has power on earth to forgive sins" (Mark 2:10).

Jesus saw His acts of healing as the expression of the mind and will of God: "I must work the works of Him who sent me" (John 9:4).

Jesus also healed to prove He was the Messiah, to usher in the Kingdom, or to confirm His messiahship (Matthew 11:3-5). Our Lord, clearly stated that one of the signs of the Kingdom in the midst of us is healing (Matthew 12:15-18; Luke 10:9).

Divine Healing

The expression "divine healing," in light of Scripture, denotes the direct ministry of God upon an afflicted body to restore it to health. Divine healing involves a direct act by God through the personal mediation of the victorious resurrected Christ. Or, as one evangelist defined it, "Divine healing is the divine power of Jesus Christ to heal the sick in answer to the prayers of His people."

Applying the Truth

MY DAILY WALK WITH GOD

We have studied the ministry of healing in both the Old and New Testaments. The objective of this section has been to research and comprehend God's provision for healing.

Fill in the Blanks

Naaman was healed when he dipped himself in the Jordan River _____ times (2 Kings 5:1-27)

By Jesus' wounds we are _____ (Isaiah 53:1-5).

Concerning the man born blind: "Neither this man nor his parents _____" (John 9:1-41).

DIVINE HEALING THROUGH SPIRITUAL GIFTS

Gifts of Healing

A Christian receives healing through gifts of healing—"to another gifts of healing by that one Spirit. . . . And in the church God has appointed . . . those having gifts of healing" (1 Corinthians 12:9, 28, *NIV*). These gifts are part of the ministry of the church.

What is "gifts of healing"? It is a manifestation of healing power from God in a supernatural way through one individual to another. The manifestations of the gifts of healing are initiated by the Holy Spirit.

All Kinds of Sickness

Notice that this is the only spiritual gift listed in the plural (gifts of healing). This is obviously due to the fact that there are so many kinds of diseases, maladies and sicknesses that many forms are required for their cure. Some are physical, some are emotional and some are mental, some are temporary and some are permanent, some are real and some are imaginary, some are common and some are rare—but all indicate a degree of distress in the human race.

It may also be listed in the plural because some people with the gift of healing are used in different gifts of healing or special areas of healings (such as deaf-mute or paralytic, etc.). Some may have a gift to heal a certain illness and others a different illness.

The Bible abounds with so many accounts of healings that it would be impossible here to list them all. Divine healing is thoroughly established in the Bible.

Agencies of Healing

The agencies of healing throughout the Bible are many. Jesus healed by putting spittle on a blind man's eyes (John 9:6, 7). The sick were healed when even the shadow of Simon Peter passed over them (Acts 5:15). Handkerchiefs or cloths anointed with oils were sent out from Paul, and those who received them were healed of their diseases (Acts 19:11, 12).

DIVINE HEALING IS FOR TODAY

Healing Today

It is God's will to heal you because healing is in His redemptive plan. Isaiah saw healing as God's provision in the future Kingdom: "The inhabitant will not say, 'I am sick'; the people who dwell in it will be forgiven their iniquity" (Isaiah 33:24). Our Lord revealed that the Kingdom is both eschatological and contemporary. It belongs to the end of the age as well as being present with us now. Our Lord clearly stated that one sign of the Kingdom in the midst of us is that "the blind receive sight, the lame walk, those who have leprosy are cured, the deaf hear, the dead are raised, and the good news is preached to the poor" (Matthew 11:5, *NIV*; see also 12:28).

Bearing Our Infirmities

"Surely He has borne our grief [infirmities] and carried our sorrows" (Isaiah 53:4). In Matthew the foregoing verse is quoted and demonstrated. There is the story of the healing of Peter's mother-in-law and then a general healing event in which Jesus cast out demons and "healed all who were sick" (Matthew 8:16). This was to fulfill what was spoken through the prophet Isaiah: "He Himself took our infirmities and bore our sicknesses" (v. 17).

By His Stripes

In 1 Peter 2:24 the work of Christ is described: "[He] Himself bore our sins in His own body on the tree, that we, having died to sins, might live for righteousness—by whose stripes you were healed."

Thus Isaiah, Matthew and Peter—three witnesses—tell us not only that Jesus shed His blood for the remissions of our sins, but that by His stripes we are healed.

Atonement

Those committed to the doctrine of divine healing generally agree that the atonement of Jesus is the ground on which divine healing rests. The words *atonement, make atonement,* and *appease* occur about 110 times in the Old Testament, principally in Leviticus and Numbers, and the root idea is "to cover." Atonement was an Old Testament feast celebrated once a year to atone for the sins of the nation. It carried the concept of reconciliation.

Today, under grace, we look back to Calvary, when the great Day of Atonement took place once and for all.

Calvary Blessing

Thus, healing is a "Calvary blessing," an integral part of the Atonement, and its appropriation is a matter of faith and not of works.

PERSONAL TESTIMONIES

Asthma

I suffered from asthma up to the age of 10. I experienced terrible attacks until I felt almost breathless. One midnight hour I suffered another attack and I cried out to my father for help. He was a Church of God minister. He prayed for my healing; the attack ceased, and I have never had another one since that time.

Healing of a Baby

I pastored in Houston, Texas. One Sunday night after church, a member from the church asked me to go to the hospital to pray for a baby who was dying. When I arrived at the hospital, I found the doctor treating the baby. I asked the doctor about the baby's condition. He said, "The mother's water bag broke and the baby drank some of the water; he has had seven heart attacks. Tell the father he is going to die." The father was not a Christian. I told him, "As long as there is life, there is hope." I prayed for the healing of the baby. Three days later the baby went home with his parents, completely healed.

HOW TO RECEIVE HEALING

Methods of Healing

There are a number of methods in the Word of God whereby healings can be obtained. There are also many causes that bring on sickness. In the case of Epaphroditus, illness came because he neglected his body (Philippians 2:30). In the Old Testament careful principles of sanitation, diet, quarantine and rest are laid down. We must follow the general laws of health and take care of our body because it is the temple of God.

Five Classifications

The Bible indicates that there are various kinds of sickness and suffering: (1) organic, such as the case of Timothy's weak stomach (1 Timothy 5:23); (2) external, such as Paul's thorn in the flesh (2 Corinthians 12:7); (3) corrective, such as leprosy upon Miriam (Numbers 12:10); (4) judicial, such as the leprosy upon Gehazi (2 Kings 5:27); and (5) inner healing, for the brokenhearted (Luke 4:18).

Brokenhearted

"To heal the brokenhearted" is a promise for inner healing—the mind, the emotions and painful memories. In medical terms this is called "psychosomatic" illness, which describes the relationship between mind and body. Through prayer we are set free from feelings of resentment, rejection, self-pity, guilt, fear, sorrow, hatred, inferiority, self-condemnation, and so forth. Even in secular circles it is widely held today that, although healing may have an organic manifestation, it has a spiritual root. Inner healing may be seen in Matthew 9:2-7, which shows Christ's healing and forgiving sins in the case of the paralytic. Both are spoken of as nearly identical acts.

STEPS FOR RECEIVING HEALING

1. Use the name of Jesus against the devil. Pray in the name of Jesus that disease and sickness leave, "If you ask anything in My name, I will do it" (John 14:13, 14).

2. Believe that healing is for you. A study of our Lord's healings reveals that nearly always He asked the sick to have faith that He would heal (Mark 9:23; Hebrews 11).

3. Learn from the faith of the Canaanite woman (Matthew 15:21-28).

   • Her faith was precise—"My daughter is severely demon-possessed."

- Her faith was patient—"[Jesus] answered her not a word."

- Her faith was persistent—"She keeps crying out" (*NIV*).

- Her faith was prudent—"Even the little dogs eat the crumbs which fall from their masters' table."

- Her faith was praised—"O woman, great is your faith!"

- Her faith was productive—"Her daughter was healed from that very hour."

4. Ask to be anointed with oil in accordance with James 5:14. The Lord heals through His body which is the church. "They will lay hands on the sick, and they will recover" (Mark 16:18).

The Devil's Power

Remember, sickness does not come from God, but from the devil—"healing all who were under the power of the devil" (Acts 10:38, *NIV*; see also 1 Corinthians 15:26).

Do not despair if you do not receive your physical healing. Healing is in the providence of God. Even though faith is exercised in a truly Scriptural way, healing does not always take place. We must also remember God does heal through natural means. Jesus said that it is the sick who need a doctor (Luke 5:31). Therefore, we pray God's mercy upon every good physician and nurse in the land. In faith we know that what men cannot do, God can do.

In God's Hands

Even when I pray and do not receive my healing immediately, I find great comfort and serenity in knowing my illness is in the hands of God.

Applying the Truth
MY DAILY WALK WITH GOD

The evidence of Scripture as it relates to sickness is that healing is part of the provision of the Atonement for our days.

True or False ___ Isaiah 33:24 explains that healing is futuristic.

True or False ___ Matthew 8:17 contradicts 1 Peter 2:24.

True or False ___ Healing is not an integral part of the atonement of Christ, because it is part of an Old Testament feast.

True or False ___ The faith of the Canaanite woman was productive.

Healing for Others

In life and all around us we are faced with much illness. This is a fact the church can't ignore. We are not only to seek our own healing but, as Jesus taught, also that of our neighbor: "I was sick and you looked after me" (Matthew 25:36, *NIV*). In view of the urgent need for healing today, and to the Bible's testimony of its divine provision, healing stands as a vital arm of the church in ministering to the needs of people.

FAITH AND DISCIPLESHIP

Faith

True discipleship will be based on faith in Jesus, "who for the joy that was set before Him endured the cross" (Hebrews 12:2). He started our life toward abundant living. He set the example. He loved us. Faith operates in love; if we love one another, God lives in us (1 John 4:12). Discipleship is created by the love of God flowing out to others. Jesus, moved with love and compassion, healed the needy (Mark 1:40, 41).

Love

Love releases true faith and compassion. For example, four men came carrying the paralytic. Seeing their faith, Jesus said, "Son, your sins are forgiven you." Those men not only brought the sick man to Jesus but, when they encountered an obstacle and could not get him to Jesus because of the crowd, they dug an opening through the roof and lowered him (Mark 2:1-12). Thus, working for the healing of our brothers and sisters is part of the ministry of the community of faith. We are partners with God for deliverance.

Mercy

Is that not also the teaching of the parable of the Good Samaritan? "He went to him and bandaged his wounds" (Luke 10:34). Did not the lack of mercy cause a rich man to wake up in hell? At his gate laid a beggar named Lazarus, covered with sores and longing to eat, and the dogs licked his sores (Luke 16:19-31).

Ministries of Healing

There are many healing ministries that the church can provide: medical missionaries, hospital visitation, nursing homes, decent housing, counseling centers, homes for abused women and children, centers for drug addicts and alcoholics, and so forth. The same God who provided for the Israelites intends that health and well-being be the basic privilege of God's people of every age. As John wrote, "I pray that you may enjoy good health and that all may go well with you, even as your soul is getting along well" (3 John 2, *NIV*).

LESSON REVIEW

After studying this lesson, what questions on divine healing did it answer for you?

After studying this lesson, what questions on divine healing did it not answer for you?

In Exodus 15:26 the Lord promises healing to the nation if they will obey Him; but in Leviticus 14 and 15 and Deuteronomy 23:9-14, He teaches them how to prevent the spread of disease. What is the lesson to be learned here?

Describe the different ways that healing is administered through the body of Christ (the church).

GROUP PROJECT

Do a community analysis to discover which is the greater healing need in your community and do a ministry project to help meet that need.

◆ Jehovah-Rapha—"The Lord who heals you" (Exodus 15:25, 26)

◆ First recorded act of healing (Genesis 20:17)

◆ Sin is the most devastating disease (Isaiah 53:4, 5).

◆ Jesus' agenda includes physical and emotional healing (Luke 4:18).

◆ Jesus commissioned others to heal the sick (Mark 16:15-18).

◆ Jesus healed that we may know He also forgives sins (Mark 2:10, 11).

◆ The gifts of healing are part of the church's ministry (1 Corinthians 12:9, 28).

◆ A sign of the Kingdom in our midst is divine healing (Matthew 11:5).

◆ Isaiah, Matthew and Peter give witness that healing is for today.

◆ Our atonement took place on calvary once and for all.

◆ "To heal the brokenhearted" is a promise for inner healing.

◆ Use the faith of the Canaanite woman

◆ Even if healing does not come initially, we have great comfort.

◆ Discipleship is created by the love of God flowing out to others.

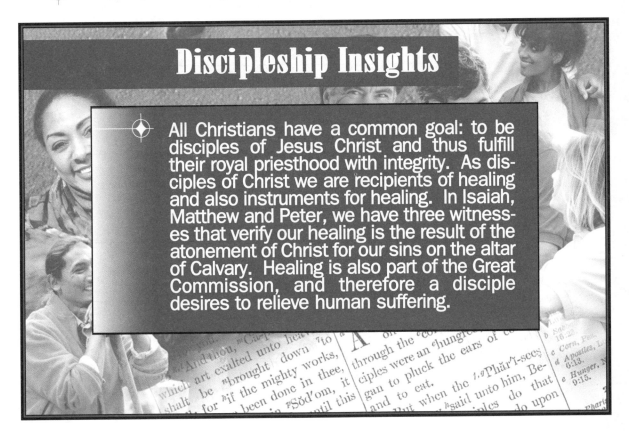

Discipleship Insights

◆ All Christians have a common goal: to be disciples of Jesus Christ and thus fulfill their royal priesthood with integrity. As disciples of Christ we are recipients of healing and also instruments for healing. In Isaiah, Matthew and Peter, we have three witnesses that verify our healing is the result of the atonement of Christ for our sins on the altar of Calvary. Healing is also part of the Great Commission, and therefore a disciple desires to relieve human suffering.

Resources

Conn, Charles W. *A Balanced Church*. Cleveland, TN: Pathway Press, 1975.

Hagin, Kenneth E. *Seven Things You Should Know About Divine Healing*. Tulsa, OK: n.p., 1983.

Thomas, Chris. *The Origin of Illness in New Testament Thought*. Sheffield, England: Sheffield Press, 1998.

NOTES:_____

_____

_____

_____

_____

_____

_____

_____

_____

_____

_____

_____

_____

_____

_____

_____

_____

_____

_____

_____

RAPTURE

Second Coming of Christ

LESSON 11

Mike L. Baker

INTRODUCTION

Throughout this lesson, the focus will be upon understanding the basic doctrine of the second coming of Jesus Christ. It will define simply various terms and elements of the doctrine, list chronologically the order of future events as described by the premillennial view, and provide insights for the believer into the "blessed hope" of Christ's return. Numerous writings are available for deeper study into the doctrine, and the student of Scripture will want to dig deeper into the multiple facets of the Second Coming.

Declaration of Faith

We believe in the premillennial second coming of Jesus. First, to resurrect the righteous dead and to catch away the living saints to Him in the air. Second, to reign on the earth a thousand years (Zechariah 14:4; 1 Corinthians 15:51, 52; 1 Thessalonians 4:14-17; 2 Thessalonians 1:7-10; 2:1; Jude 14, 15; Revelation 5:10; 19:11-21; 20:4-6).

Article 13

Scriptural Focus

> **A**nd if I go and prepare a place for you, I will come again and receive you to Myself; that where I am, there you may be also.

John 14:3

What about the future? Prophecy is one of the most vibrant and fascinating doctrines of the church. It is a subject described as "dealing with things to come," "details of end-time events," "the coming Apocalypse," "the consummation of the age," "the order of future events," "the end of the world," "the earth's final days," and many other descriptions. So, what is prophecy? Prophecy is the prediction of the future under the influence of divine guidance. It is the declaration of the will of God, both present and future. God chose to bring His message through individuals called prophets. A prophet is a spokesman of God's special revelation, and prophecy, in its broadest sense, is simply the message of a prophet.

God the Healer

During the time of Jesus, the Jewish people wanted to know what the future held. They longed for the coming Messiah and they knew that when He came, He would overthrow their oppressors and make things right. He would establish the kingdom in Israel and fulfill God's promise of peace. Today, there is a strong impression both among Christians and non-Christians that we are approaching the end of the world and people want to know about the future. They are interested in eschatology.

First Healing

ESCHATOLOGY

Eschatology is translated from the Greek word *eschatos,* meaning "farthest or the last thing." Eschatology is simply the study of the end times or last days.

Eschatology

The expression "thousand years" occurs six times in Revelation 20:1-7. This expression gave rise to the term *millennium. Millennium* comes from the Latin *mille,* meaning "thousand," and *annus,* meaning "year." The Millennium is the period of a thousand years during which Christ will reign on earth with peace and prevailing righteousness. This is frequently referred to as the "millennial reign."

Millennium

PREMILLENNIALISM

There are three major eschatological views regarding the order of future events. **Premillennialism** is the view that the second coming of Christ to the earth and the

Eschatological Views

establishment of His kingdom of peace and righteousness will take place before the thousand years' reign. The term *premillennial* is made up of three Latin elements: *pre* means "before," *mille* means "thousand," and *annus* means "year." Premillennialism means simply that Christ will return to earth "before the thousand years." **Amillennialism** is the view that when Christ returns, eternity begins with no prior millennial (thousand-year) reign on earth. The **postmillennial** view holds that through the church's influence the world will be Christianized before Christ returns. This view believes that immediately following His return, eternity begins.

Church of God—Premillenial

It is generally agreed by students of the early church that premillennialism is the oldest of the three millennial views and was the view held by many in the post-apostolic age. It is a doctrine not held by any certain church, denomination or sect, but is held by many Protestant Evangelical churches. The Church of God believes in the premillennial second coming of Jesus Christ. This conveys the belief that there will be a literal thousand-year reign of Jesus Christ upon the earth following the events of the Rapture, Tribulation and Second Coming.

PROPHETICAL REFERENCES

The Old Testament is replete with references to the Second Coming. Isaiah describes the acceptable year of the Lord and the day of vengeance: "The Spirit of the Lord God is upon Me, because the Lord has anointed Me to preach good tidings to the poor; He has sent Me to heal the brokenhearted, to proclaim liberty to the captives, and the opening of the prison to those who are bound; to proclaim the acceptable year of the Lord, and the day of vengeance of our God; to comfort all who mourn" (61:1, 2; see also Daniel 2:44, 45; Zechariah 14:1-4; Malachi 3:1).

New Testament References

The New Testament provides more than 300 references to Christ's coming to resurrect and rapture the church or to His return to the earth to set up His kingdom. The apostle Paul referred to the Second Coming at least 50 times.

In Matthew 24:3, the disciples came to Jesus as He sat on the Mount of Olives and said, "Tell us, when will these things be? And what will be the sign of Your coming, and of the end of the age?"

Signs of His Coming

Jesus responded to the disciples' questions by describing in verses 4-14 various signs that will precede His second coming. These signs include: those who claim to be Christ (v. 5), deception (v. 5), wars and rumors of wars (v. 6), nation rising against nation (v. 7), famine and earthquakes (v. 7), an abundance of false prophets (v. 11), love growing cold (v. 12), and the gospel being preached in all the world (v. 14).

In John 14:1-3, Jesus testified of His second coming: "Let not your heart be troubled; you believe in God, believe also in Me. In My Father's house are many mansions; if it were not so, I would have told you. I go to prepare a place for you. And if I go and prepare a place for you, I will come again and receive you to Myself; that where I am, there you may be also."

Throughout the New Testament the apostles bore witness to His second coming (Hebrews 9:28; 1 John 2:28; Jude 14, 15). In Acts 3:20, 21, Luke said, "And that He may send Jesus Christ, who was preached to you before, whom heaven must receive until the times of restoration of all things, which God has spoken by the mouth of all His holy prophets since the world began." In Titus 2:13, Paul tells us why the Second Coming is so very important—it is the hope of the church, and with anticipation we are "looking for the blessed hope and glorious appearing of our great God and Savior Jesus Christ."

Applying the Truth
MY DAILY WALK WITH GOD

 Match the following definitions with their respective term:

The view or study of the end times or last days.	Premillennialism
The view that believes that through the church's influence the world will be Christianized before Christ returns.	Eschatology
The view that the second coming of Christ to the earth and the establishment of His kingdom of peace and righteousness will take place before the thousand years' reign.	Amillennialism
The view that when Christ returns, eternity begins with no prior millennial reign on earth.	Postmillennial

ORDER OF EVENTS

The Church of God believes in Christ's imminent return, that is, He could come at any time. His coming will be the fulfillment of the promise of the prophets and Christ himself. Premillennialists are generally in agreement on the order of major events in the future.

Christ's Imminent Return

The following list provides an order of future events according to the premillennial view:

Order of Future Events

1. The Rapture. This event is the resurrection of the dead in Christ accompanied by the translation of the living saints (1 Corinthians 15:20-24, 35-52; 1 Thessalonians 4:13-18). Christ comes for His saints, and this is called the first resurrection.

2. The Great Tribulation. The Tribulation is a seven-year period of intense suffering and divine judgment (Revelation 6—19). Those raptured (resurrected and translated) are with the Lord in heaven. The judgment seat of Christ (1 Corinthians 3:12-15) and the marriage of the Lamb take place (Revelation 19:7) while the Tribulation judgments are poured out on earth.

3. The Second Coming of Christ. Christ comes with His own in glory to establish the millennial kingdom (Revelation 19:11-16).

4. The Battle of Armageddon. This is the appointed place where the armies of the Beast (Antichrist) and the False Prophet will be destroyed by Christ's descending to earth with power and glory (Revelation 19:17-21).

5. Judgment of Israel and the Gentile Nations. When Christ comes, Israel will be regathered and judged and the Gentile nations will also be judged (Matthew 24:37—25:46).

6. The Millennial Reign. The reign of Christ will be 1,000 years (Revelation 20:1-6). However, before it begins Satan is bound and cast into the bottomless pit during the thousand years (vv. 20:1-3). At the end of the thousand years' reign, Satan will be loosed for a little season (v. 7). He will deceive the nations and lead a revolt against God, be defeated by Christ, and cast into the lake of fire and brimstone where he will remain forever (vv. 8-10).

7. Great White Throne Judgment. At this event the wicked dead of all the ages are resurrected (referred to as the second resurrection), judged and cast into the lake of fire (Revelation 20:11-15).

8. Creation of the New Heaven, New Earth and New Jerusalem. The first heaven and earth are passed away and God creates a new heaven, earth and Jerusalem as the dwelling place throughout eternity for the saints of all ages (Revelation 21:1, 2).

9. Eternity (Revelation 22).

Applying the Truth
MY DAILY WALK WITH GOD

Why do I need to know the importance of studying the order of future events?

If I don't understand the second coming of Christ and the order of future events . . .

- I may not understand that Jesus is coming again and that I need to be ready.

- I may not be motivated to share the message of His coming with others.

- I may neglect my Bible study and not see the purpose of God's revelation for me.

- I may miss the assurance that He is in control, that He loves me and He will take care of me regardless what the future holds.

- Knowing God's plan for the future stirs us to holy living in preparation of meeting Christ when He returns.

THE RAPTURE OF THE CHURCH

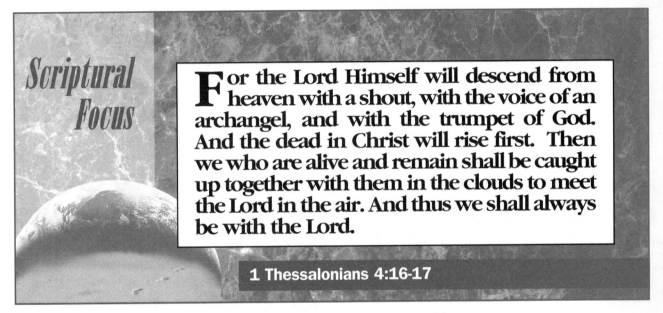

Scriptural Focus

For the Lord Himself will descend from heaven with a shout, with the voice of an archangel, and with the trumpet of God. And the dead in Christ will rise first. Then we who are alive and remain shall be caught up together with them in the clouds to meet the Lord in the air. And thus we shall always be with the Lord.

1 Thessalonians 4:16-17

The second coming of Christ is one advent that takes place with two events or phases. Christ will first come to rapture the church (first event) and then, when the Tribulation period is finished, Christ will come to the earth with His saints to establish His kingdom upon the earth (second event). The coming for His own is called the "Rapture"; Christ's coming with His own is called the "Second Coming."

Coming *for*
Coming *With*

CHRIST'S COMING IN THE AIR

The Church of God believes the Rapture can occur at any moment and that Christians should be constantly watching and anticipating Christ's return. The word *rapture* does not appear in the Bible. While this is true, Latin translators of the Greek New Testament used the word *rapere,* meaning "to snatch, seize or catch away suddenly." Many of contemporary theological terms have been derived from a Latin base. *Rapture* is such a word.

Rapture defined

First Thessalonians 4:17 teaches the fact of the Rapture: "We . . . shall be caught up together with them in the clouds." The English phrase "caught up" translates from the Greek word *harpazo*, which means "to seize upon with force" or "to snatch up." It is accurately rendered into English by "caught up." In 1 Corinthians 15:52, Paul describes this catching away as happening "in a moment, in the twinkling of an eye."

The Rapture is Christ's coming in the air, not for the people who belong to the world but for those who have looked forward to and prepared for His coming. Luke 12:40 lets us know clearly that no one knows the day or the hour of Christ's coming: "Therefore you also be ready, for the Son of Man is coming at an hour you do not expect." Jesus, the Bridegroom, will come and take away His bride, the church.

Christ's feet do not touch the earth at the Rapture. First Thessalonians 4:16, 17 says the dead in Christ will rise all at once and meet Him in the air with resurrected bodies. Those who are living will be changed in a moment and also join with Christ and the resurrected in the air.

Impact of the Rapture

The Rapture is the only conceivable event that could cause the entire world to unite in a new world government and religion. With millions removed from the earth there will exist a moral and spiritual vacuum that will cause the world to submit to the leadership of the Antichrist as the world dictator. To prepare the world to embrace the Antichrist, it will require an extraordinary event—the Rapture. The disruption on a global scale would be beyond calculation. Professing Christians hold key positions everywhere in the world. Their disappearance would cause many nations to teeter on the brink of disaster and collapse. All mankind will share the bewilderment and consternation of worldwide devastation.

THE GREAT TRIBULATION

Daniel's "Seventy Weeks"

The Great Tribulation is the seven-year period between the rapture of the church and the second coming of Christ. In Revelation 6—19, John provides a detailed exposition of the Tribulation. Daniel's "seventy weeks" is the framework within which the Tribulation, or the Seventieth Week, occurs (Daniel 9:24-27). The "seventy weeks" of the prophecy are understood by most scholars to be weeks of years. Seventy "sevens" of years represents 490 years in which great events take place in relation to Jerusalem and the Jewish people.

The first two major time segments involved 483 years, or 69 "sevens." The first segment began with the decree to restore and rebuild Jerusalem given to Nehemiah in 445 B.C. (49 years). The second time segment of 62 weeks (434 years) marked the time that would pass until the Messiah was cut off. The 483 years of 69 "sevens" ended when Christ was crucified.

One week of seven years remains still unfulfilled. Following the Rapture and at the beginning of the peace covenant negotiated by the Antichrist, the last seven years of the predicted 490 will be complete.

Tribulation Period

In Matthew 24:4-28, Jesus describes the Tribulation period. In verses 4-14, He speaks about the first half of the Tribulation, and in verses 15-28, He describes the second half leading up to the Second Coming. The prophet Joel wrote: "Blow the trumpet in Zion, and sound an alarm in My holy mountain! Let all the inhabitants of the land tremble; for the day of the Lord is coming, for it is at hand: A day of darkness and gloominess, a day of clouds and thick darkness, like the morning clouds spread over the mountains. A people come, great and strong, the like of whom has never been; nor will there ever be any such after them, even for many successive generations" (Joel 2:1, 2).

The Tribulation is divided into two parts: the first three and one-half years, which is a time of relative calm, and the last three and one-half years, which is a time of calamity.

Series of Judgments

The Book of Revelation describes a series of three judgments of God. These include the following:

- ◈ The Seven Seals (Revelation 6)
- ◈ The Seven Trumpets (Revelation 8 and 9)
- ◈ The Seven Bowls of Wrath (Revelation 16)

THE ANTICHRIST

Identifying the Antichrist

The Antichrist is the individual who arises during the Tribulation and gains worldwide power for three and one-half years. In 1 John 2:22, he is referred to as "antichrist." While he is discussed extensively in the Scriptures, he is referred to by many other references. Some of these identifications include the following:

- ◈ "The prince who is to come" (Daniel 9:26)
- ◈ "The abomination of desolation" (Matthew 24:15; Daniel 9:27)
- ◈ "The son of perdition" (2 Thessalonians 2:3)
- ◈ "The beast" (Revelation 11:7; 13:1; 14:9; 15:2; 16:2; 17:3, 13; 19:20; 20:10)

The term "antichrist" has become a widely used identification by students of prophecy throughout church history.

Antichrist's Ascension to Power

After Christ returns and raptures the church from the earth, the Antichrist will ascend to power as the leader of a confederation of 10 nations (Daniel 7:24, 25). This confederation is symbolized as a beast with 10 horns and represents an international political entity. The Antichrist will forcibly take control of the confederation. While he emerges as a political leader, he will gradually acquire religious connotations and require those subject to him to worship him (2 Thessalonians 2:4). He will be active throughout all of the Tribulation; however, for three and one-half years he will persecute Christians and other opponents in a reign of terror.

The False Prophet

The Antichrist and the False Prophet are two separate individuals who work toward a common goal of deception. The False Prophet is a prophet or spokesman for the Antichrist. He is depicted as one who uses religion and signs and wonders to deceive the masses into worshiping the Antichrist.

When Christ returns, the power and rule of the Antichrist will terminate at the Battle of Armageddon. He and the False Prophet will be judged and cast alive into the lake of fire (Revelation 19:20).

Applying the Truth
MY DAILY WALK WITH GOD

For Thought and Discussion:

How much thought have you given to the Rapture? _____ _____ Have you ever thought that the world might come to an end? _____

When you think about the possibility of Christ's coming back to earth in your lifetime, does it cause you to want to live differently?

_____

_____

What areas of your life would you change if you knew the Rapture would take place today? _____

_____

_____

_____

_____

_____

_____

Can you imagine what it will be like on earth to go through the Tribulation? _____

_____

_____

_____

_____

Scriptural Focus

Immediately after the tribulation of those days the sun will be darkened, and the moon will not give its light; the stars will fall from heaven, and the powers of the heavens will be shaken. Then the sign of the Son of Man will appear in heaven, and then all the tribes of the earth will mourn, and they will see the Son of Man coming on the clouds of heaven with power and great glory. And He will send His angels with a great sound of a trumpet, and they will gather together His elect from the four winds, from one end of heaven to the other.

Matthew 24:29-31

The second coming of Christ is not His coming in the air but His coming to earth after the Great Tribulation. It is one of the major events in the Bible, and everyone will witness His return. It will end the Tribulation and usher in the Millennium.

Dramatic Event

When Jesus first came to earth, He was born in a humble stable, relatively unnoticed by mankind. The second coming of Christ to earth will be the most dramatic and decisive event in the history of the world. His return in power and glory will capture the attention of every nation and the total of humanity.

Description of Christ's Coming

The most detailed description of the Second Coming is found in Revelation 19:11-16:

Now I saw heaven opened, and behold, a white horse. And He who sat on him was called Faithful and True, and in righteousness He judges and makes war. His eyes were like a flame of fire, and on His head were many crowns. He had a name written that no one knew except Himself. He was clothed with a robe dipped in blood, and His name is called The Word of God. And the armies in heaven, clothed in fine linen, white and clean, followed Him on white horses. Now out of His mouth goes a sharp sword, that with it He should strike the nations. And He Himself will rule them with a rod of iron. He Himself treads the winepress of the fierceness and wrath of Almighty God. And He has on His robe and on His thigh a name written: KING OF KINGS AND LORD OF LORDS.

As fighting armies pause in their conflict with each other, the heavens will open and Christ will begin the majestic procession from heaven to earth. This spectacle will be awesome as millions of saints and angels reflecting the glory of God and led by Christ astride a white horse, a symbol of a conqueror, ascend to earth.

Geological Reaction

Zechariah 14:4 describes the dramatic geological reaction to Christ's physical presence as He stands on the Mount of Olives: "And in that day His feet will stand on the Mount of Olives, which faces Jerusalem on the east. And the Mount of Olives shall be split in two, from east to west, making a very large valley; half of the mountain shall move toward the north and half of it toward the south." The Mount of Olives will be divided and a great valley will stretch out into the Jordan Valley below.

The Second Coming is when Christ returns to earth to defeat the Antichrist and judge all the world's unbelievers.

THE BATTLE OF ARMAGEDDON

Megiddo

The term *Armageddon* comes from the Hebrew language and is referenced in Revelation 16:16, "And they gathered them together to the place called in Hebrew, Armageddon." The term is generally interpreted as meaning the mountain of Megiddo. Megiddo is located on the north side of the plains of Jezreel. It is an ancient city that overlooks the Valley Esdraelon in northern Israel.

The Battle

According to the Scriptures, great armies from the east and the west will gather and assemble on the plains at Megiddo. The Antichrist will be threatened from the south and he will move to destroy a revived Babylon in the east. He will finally turn his forces toward Jerusalem to conquer and destroy it. As his armies move on Jerusalem, Jesus Christ returns to rescue Israel. Christ and His angelic army will destroy the armies of the Antichrist, capture him, and cast him and the False Prophet into the lake of fire (Revelation 19:20).

THE MILLENNIAL REIGN

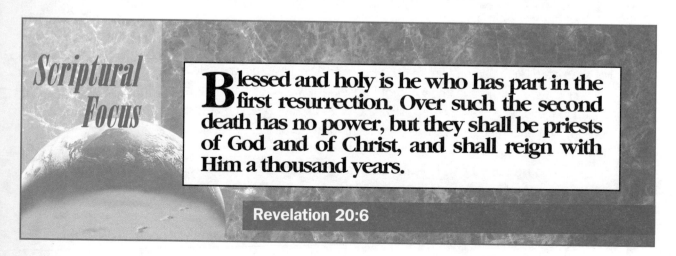

Scriptural Focus

Blessed and holy is he who has part in the first resurrection. Over such the second death has no power, but they shall be priests of God and of Christ, and shall reign with Him a thousand years.

Revelation 20:6

The Millennium is a thousand years' period when Christ will reign upon the earth following His second coming. It will be a time of universal peace, prosperity, long life and prevailing righteousness. Christ will establish His kingdom and set up His throne in the city of Jerusalem. He will reign and rule visibly over the world in power and glory, ensuring equity and justice for all.

Millennium Reign

At the end of the Tribulation, Satan will be bound and cast into the bottomless pit and "shut up, and a seal will be set on him, so that he should deceive the nations no more till the thousand years are finished" (see Revelation 20:3). Satan is not simply restricted; he is totally inactive during the Millennium and reign of Christ.

Satan Bound

What will the Millennium be like for the people of God? The Millennium will be a reward for the people of God. It will redeem creation following the devastation of the Tribulation and make it new and beautiful once more. Isaiah 2:1-4 describes the coming kingdom as peaceful when people will "beat their swords into plowshares, and their spears into pruning hooks." Nations will not lift their weapons against each other in war. It will be a time of good news, and fear will be a thing of the past. Isaiah 11:6-9 describes a scene of animals so tame that they will be docile to humans and each other. Sickness and infirmity will be virtually removed and no one will live in poverty. It will be a time of prosperity and great personal joy, and believers will rule with Christ.

Millenium Described

At the end of the Millennium, Satan will be released and will go out to deceive the nations and rebel against the millennial reign of Christ. In one final grasp for power, he will attempt to seize the throne of God. Satan's defeat and termination comes to a swift judgment. He is cast into the lake of fire to be tormented forever and ever.

Satan Released

GREAT WHITE THRONE JUDGMENT

The Great White Throne pertains to the judgment of the unbelieving dead as recorded in Revelation 20:11, 12:

> Then I saw a great white throne and Him who sat on it, from whose face the earth and the heaven fled away. And there was found no place for them. And I saw the dead, small and great, standing before God, and books were opened. And another book was opened, which is the Book of Life. And the dead were judged according to their works, by the things which were written in the books.

This is known as the second resurrection. The wicked dead are resurrected and the "Book of Life" is opened. This book is opened as a proof to those who are being judged that they are unworthy of eternal life. This judgment will occur at the end of the Millennium. It is not a general judgment where both the righteous and the wicked shall stand before God, but is a judgment of the wicked dead. They are there because they have rejected Christ during their lifetimes. Their works are judged to show that the punishment is deserved. It is a throne of sentence and pronounces a verdict of eternal punishment in the lake of fire. It is the final judgment.

Second Ressurection— Wicked Dead

In Revelation 21:1, 2, John writes: "Now I saw a new heaven and a new earth, for the first heaven and the first earth had passed away. Also there was no more sea. Then I, John, saw the holy city, New Jerusalem, coming down out of heaven from God, prepared as a bride adorned for her husband." Following the Millennium, the present earth will be destroyed so that all the effect of sin will be eradicated (2 Peter 3:10-12). God will then create a new heaven and earth to remain throughout eternity.

Dwelling Place of the Redeemed

After the present earth has been destroyed, the New Jerusalem will descend from heaven and continue throughout eternity as the dwelling place of the redeemed who will serve God forever. This city will be unlike any the world has ever known. It will be a picture of maximum beauty made of the most lavish materials such as diamonds, emeralds and streets paved with gold. As a believer in Christ, this will be your home for eternity.

Applying the Truth
MY DAILY WALK WITH GOD

For Thought and Discussion:

◆ Take time to examine your life and look for anything that may keep you from focusing on Christ's second coming. _____

_____

_____

◆ When people see trouble in the world around them and are alarmed, what can you say to them regarding the coming of Christ, the millennial reign and judgment? _____

_____

_____

◆ In what ways are the Rapture and the Second Coming distinct from each other? _____

_____

_____

What level of personal confidence do you have in your understanding of the second coming of Christ and prophetical future events?

_____

THE BELIEVER'S HOPE

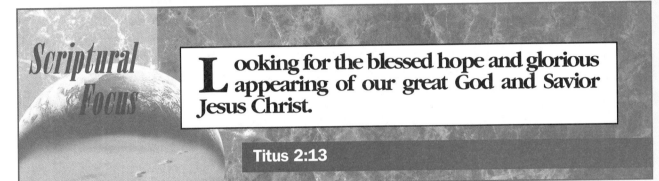

Scriptural Focus

Looking for the blessed hope and glorious appearing of our great God and Savior Jesus Christ.

Titus 2:13

Our "Blessed Hope"

The first coming of Christ to this earth gave us the hope of eternal life. Through the sacrifice of His life, the gift of His love and the power of His resurrection we have the promise of salvation and reconciliation to God. In Titus 2:13, the coming of the Lord is presented as our "blessed hope" for the future. The ultimate hope of the Christian is Christ's return.

Hope of the World

The question is asked again, What about the future? It is a future of expectancy and confidence in the completion of God's promises. It is His second coming: first, to resurrect the righteous dead and to catch away the living saints to Him in the air, and second, to reign on the earth a thousand years. His return is the believer's hope—it is the hope of the world.

Are you ready for the events of the future? Will you be raptured with the Lord's people and go into His presence? As a Christian, we are to be looking for that "blessed hope"—the coming of Jesus Christ—and growing in His love and living in the Holy Spirit.

LESSON REVIEW

What about the future? Prophecy is one of the most vibrant and fascinating doctrines of the church. It is the prediction of the future under the influence of divine guidance. It is the declaration of the will of God, both present and future. Eschatology is the study of the end times or last days.

Millennium is the period of a thousand years during which Christ will reign on earth with peace and prevailing righteousness. Premillennialism is the view that the second coming of Christ to the earth and the establishment of His kingdom will take place before the thousand years' reign. The Church of God believes in the pre-millennial second coming of Christ.

The Church of God believes in Christ's imminent return. According to the pre-millennial view, the order of future events includes the following: the Rapture; Great Tribulation; second coming of Christ; Battle of Armageddon; judgment of Israel and the gentile nations; millennial reign; Great White Throne Judgment; creation of the new heaven, new earth and New Jerusalem; and eternity.

The Rapture is Christ's coming in the air for those who have looked forward to His coming. The Great Tribulation is the seven-year period between the rapture of the church and the second coming of Christ. The Antichrist is the individual who arises during the Tribulation and gains worldwide power for three and one-half years. When Christ returns, the power and rule of the Antichrist will terminate at the Battle of Armageddon.

The second coming of Christ is His coming to earth after the Tribulation. He returns in power and glory, defeats the Antichrist and reigns for a thousand years. The millennial reign will be a time of universal peace and prevailing righteousness. Christ will establish His kingdom and set up His throne in the city of Jerusalem. Satan will be bound and cast into the bottomless pit for the entire Millennium.

The Great White Throne Judgment is known as the second resurrection. All of the wicked dead are resurrected and judged by their works. It is a throne of sentence and pronounces a verdict of eternal punishment.

Following the Millennium, the present earth will be destroyed so that all the effects of sin will be eradicated. God will create a new heaven and earth to remain throughout eternity. The New Jerusalem will descend from heaven and continue eternally as the dwelling place of the redeemed.

The ultimate hope of the Christian is Christ's return. It is the hope of the world.

Discipleship Insights

- Prophecy is the prediction of the future under the influence of divine guidance. It is the declaration of the will of God, both present and future.

- Premillennialism is the view that the second coming of Christ to the earth and the establishment of His kingdom of peace and righteousness will take place before the thousand years' reign. The Church of God believes in the premillennial view.

- The New Testament provides more than 300 references to Christ's coming.

- The order of future events includes the following: the Rapture; Great Tribulation; second coming of Christ; Battle of Armageddon; judgment of Israel and the gentile nations; millennial reign; Great White Throne Judgment; creation of the new heaven, new earth and New Jerusalem; and eternity.

- The coming of Christ for His saints is called the "Rapture." Christ's coming with His own is called the "Second Coming."

- The Great Tribulation is the seven-year period between the rapture of the church and the second coming of Christ.

- The second coming of Christ is after the Tribulation. His return in power and glory will capture the attention of every nation and the total of humanity.

- The millennial reign is a thousand years' period when Christ will reign upon the earth following His second coming. It will be a time of universal peace and prevailing righteousness.

- The ultimate hope of the Christian is Christ's return. It is the hope of the world.

Resources

Anders, Max. *What You Need to Know About Bible Prophecy.* Nashville: Thomas Nelson Publishers, 1997.

Arrington, French L. *Christian Doctrine: A Pentecostal Perspective*, Vol. 3. Cleveland, TN: Pathway Press, 1994.

Buxton, Clyne W. *End Times: A Biblical Study of Current and Future Events.* Cleveland, TN: Pathway Press, 1993.

Cho, David Yonggi. *The Apocalyptic Prophecy: Reconciling Today's Global Events With End-Time Prophecy.* Orlando, FL: Creation House, 1998.

Cooper, David C. *Apocalypse! A New Look at the Book of Revelation.* Cleveland, TN: Pathway Press, 1999.

Ice, Thomas, and Timothy Demy. *Fast Facts on Bible Prophecy.* Eugene, OR: Harvest House Publishers, 1997.

Lightner, Robert P. *The Last Days Handbook.* Nashville: Thomas Nelson Publishers, 1990.

MacArthur, John Jr. *Signs of Christ's Return.* Chicago: Moody Press, 1987.

Payne, J. Barton. *Encyclopedia of Biblical Prophecy.* Grand Rapids: Baker Book House, rep. ed., 1980.

Pentecost, J. Dwight. *Things to Come.* Grand Rapids: Zondervan Publishing Co., 1958.

Sims, John A. *Our Pentecostal Heritage.* Cleveland, TN: Pathway Press, 1995.

Slay, James L. *This We Believe.* Cleveland, TN: Pathway Press, 1996.

Vine, W.E. *Vine's Expository Dictionary of Old and New Testament Words.* Old Tappan, NJ: Fleming H. Revell Co., 1981.

Walvoord, John F. *The Rapture Question.* Grand Rapids: Zondervan Publishing Co., 1979.

NOTES:_____

_____

_____

_____

_____

_____

_____

RESURRECTION

The Bodily Resurrection

LESSON 12

Bill George

INTRODUCTION

The doctrine of the Resurrection is the bedrock of Christian faith.

The apostle Paul rightly declared to the Corinthian believers, "For if the dead do not rise, then Christ is not risen. And if Christ is not risen, your faith is futile; you are still in your sins! Then also those who have fallen asleep in Christ have perished. If in this life only we have hope in Christ, we are of all men the most pitiable" (1 Corinthians 15:16-19).

Resurrection

Resurrection means "the return of life to that in which life no longer exists." It means that when a person dies, whether righteous or evil, that person will be brought back to life in the future, either to receive the rewards of the just or to face the judgment of the unjust.

Purpose

The purpose of this study is to examine the Scriptural teachings concerning the 14th article of the Church of God Declaration of Faith, our belief in the bodily resurrection. When you have completed the lesson, you will be prepared to explain what the Bible says about resurrection and you will be able to rejoice in hope of the future that God has planned for you.

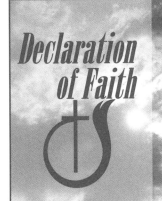

Declaration of Faith

We believe in the bodily resurrection; eternal life for the righteous, and eternal punishment for the wicked (Job 19:25-27; Daniel 12:2; John 5:21, 28, 29; 1 Corinthians 15:22, 23; Acts 24:15; Revelations 20:5, 6).

Article 14

Scriptural Focus

Your dead shall live; together with my dead body they shall arise. Awake and sing, you who dwell in dust; for your dew is like the dew of herbs, and the earth shall cast out the dead (Isaiah 26:19).

Do not marvel at this; for the hour is coming in which all who are in the graves will hear His voice and come forth—those who have done good, to the resurrection of life, and those who have done evil, to the resurrection of condemnation (John 5:28, 29).

Isaiah 26:19 ✦ John 5:28, 29

WHAT THE BIBLE TEACHES

In both the Old Testament and the New Testament the bodily resurrection is taught.

The Old Testament doesn't go into detail about the circumstances or form of the resurrected body, but the ancient book of **Job** states clearly that it will be a fleshly body—"In my flesh I shall see God" (19:26). He indicates that he will see his Redeemer *standing*; this suggests a material being. He says that he will *see* his Redeemer; this suggests that he, too, will have a body.

Old Testament

Daniel affirms that the dead, even though their bodies have turned to dust, will arise and will possess conscious understanding (see Daniel 12:2).

Isaiah predicted the resurrection, when in 26:19 he writes, "Your dead shall live."

The New Testament places great emphasis upon the resurrection. It is a theme to which **Jesus** often returns. See the following examples:

- Luke 14:13, 14. He assures that justice will be done in the resurrection.
- Luke 20:35, 36. He speaks of the character of the resurrected life in heaven.
- John 5:28, 29. He clearly foretells the resurrection of those in the grave.
- John 11:25. He says that those who believe in Him, though they may die, will live.
- John 11:41-44. He raises Lazarus as a practical demonstration of resurrection power.
- John 14:1-3. He explains that He will prepare a place and return for His people.
- John 14:19. He declares, "Because I live, you will live also."

It is a theme visited by **Paul** on numerous occasions:

- 1 Corinthians 15. Much of the chapter deals with issues pertaining to resurrection.
- Philippians 3:11. He speaks of attaining the resurrection of the dead.
- 1 Thessalonians 4:13-18. The dead in Christ will rise first.

Others mention the fact of the resurrection:

- Peter, in 1 Peter 1:3. Our resurrection is prefigured by Christ's own resurrection.
- John, in Revelation 20:4-6, 13, 14. His vision shows resurrection in two phases.

The scriptures cited here are representative of others that deal with resurrection. All readers of the Bible can affirm that it is a prominent theme that recurs again and again.

Applying the Truth
MY DAILY WALK WITH GOD

Spend a few minutes reading 1 Corinthians 15, Paul's main discussion of the resurrection, then answer the following questions:

What are some of the evidences for Christ's resurrection, according to verses 5-8? _____

_____

_____

_____

_____

WHO WILL EXPERIENCE RESURRECTION?

Several false views of the resurrection have arisen during the centuries of Christian history. One ancient heresy stated that only Christians would be resurrected; ungodly people would cease to exist when they died. Another erroneous view claimed that only the soul would rise; the body would return to dust and never be seen again.

False Theories

The Bible teaches that every person who has ever lived and died will come back to life by resurrection power and will appear in bodily form.

All Will Live

The John 5:28, 29 passage, cited above, reveals that "all who are in the graves will hear His voice and come forth."

In his 1 Corinthians 15 resurrection treatise, Paul makes it clear in verse 22 that "as in Adam all die, even so in Christ all shall be made alive."

Testifying before Felix, Paul explained that part of the reason he had been accused by the Jews in Jerusalem was his firm conviction that the resurrection was a reality. "I have hope in God, which they themselves also accept, that there will be a resurrection of the dead, both of the just and the unjust" (Acts 24:15).

Both the just and unjust will experience bodily renewal. The Scriptures indicate two phases, or perhaps better said, two resurrections. The first, the resurrection of life, will happen when Christ appears to catch away His church (1 Thessalonians 4:13-18). At that time the righteous dead will come back to life with glorified, immortal bodies. They will be given their rewards by the Son of God and will enter into the joy of the Lord.

Two Resurrections

The unrighteous dead do not come back to life at the same time. Their resurrection occurs later, according to Revelation 20:13, at the time of judgment, when "the sea gave up the dead who were in it, and Death and Hades delivered up the dead who were in them. And they were judged, each one according to his works."

"Blessed and holy is he who has part in the first resurrection," John penned in Revelation 20:6.

Applying the Truth
MY DAILY WALK WITH GOD

Who is the Christian person closest to you whom you recall dying?

_____

How were you affected by this death? _____

_____

_____

_____

_____

How do Paul's words in 1 Thessalonians 4:13-18 affect you?

_____

_____

_____

_____

What would you say to a person grieving the death of a Christian loved one that might be of comfort to him/her? _____

_____

_____

_____

_____

Like the ancient heretics, some people today do not have a correct understanding of resurrection and wrongly believe that a person who dies ceases to exist for all eternity. What scriptures would you use to show the reality of resurrection? _____

_____

_____

HOW WILL RESURRECTION OCCUR?

Mystery

Much about the resurrection remains mysterious. Except for Paul's lengthy discussion in 1 Corinthians 15, no detailed development of the doctrine exists in a single place in Scripture. By investigating the various references scattered throughout the Bible, we can put together a general explanation of it.

Fleshly

The resurrection will be bodily, fleshly. Nowhere in Scripture do we read of a resurrection that does not have the whole man in view—body, soul and spirit. The Biblical view of man is at odds with the Greek view that contended that man is a bipartite being, constituted of body and soul, and that at death the body—which during life had been something like a prison house of the soul—would perish forever, setting the soul free.

Reunited

Christians understand that in the resurrection the spirit will be reunited with a body. To the human mind this presents problems. Many bodies have been destroyed. Bodies decay; given the right circumstances, even the bones revert to dust. Some bodies are cremated, and only ashes remain. How will God bring about a reunion given these conditions?

The Bible does not explain the precise "how" of it. Paul examines the puzzling issue: "But someone will say, 'How are the dead raised up? And with what body do they come?' Foolish one, what you sow is not made alive unless it dies. And what you sow, you do not sow that body that shall be, but mere grain—perhaps wheat or some other grain. But God gives it a body as He pleases, and to each seed its own body" (1 Corinthians 15:35-38).

Same Thing

A grain of wheat is the body that is planted, according to Paul's analogy; the body that appears as a result of that seed being planted is a wheat plant. In a sense, it is not the same thing that went into the earth; in another sense, it is the same thing, but in a different form. How God will take a body that is buried (or cremated, or lost at sea, or whatever) and unite it with the departed spirit is beyond our grasp. The fact is, however, the One who created man originally from the earth and breathed into his body the breath of life will not be confronted with difficulty in uniting spirit with flesh in the resurrection.

WHAT WILL THE RESURRECTION BODY BE LIKE?

Relationship

Again, all of our questions are not answered outright. That it will have some sort of relationship with our previous body seems clear. Just as in Paul's illustration the kind of grain that appears depends on the kind of seed that is sown, it seems that the new body will have some relationship to the body that previously existed. We cannot be dogmatic at this point. Those who insist that it will be identical to the body that existed on earth base their opinion primarily on the fact that Christ's resurrected body appeared to be the same as before His death.

Christ the Model

Christ's coming back in His body is the model for our belief in resurrection. A nonmaterial Christ would not have evidential value for the resurrection. The writers of the New Testament, guided by the Holy Spirit, made much of His bodily appearances. Luke offered the appearances as "many convincing proofs" (Acts 1:3, *NIV*). An immaterial body would have no verifiable connection with a physical body. Those who saw Christ after His resurrection could know that Christ rose from the dead because He rose in the same body in which He died.

Differences

It also seems apparent that there will be essential differences between the body that died and the resurrection body. Though it will certainly be flesh, it may not be subject to the limitations of the flesh as we know it. Again, Jesus' experience becomes our anticipation. His resurrected body bore the scars afflicted by the Crucifixion. He identified Himself as flesh and blood. Luke, a physician and writer of the Gospel that bears his name, took care to emphasize the fleshly aspect: "Behold My hands and My feet, that it is I Myself. Handle Me and see, for a spirit does not have flesh and bones as you see I have" (24:39). He ate several meals with the disciples. But ostensibly He could enter a room without walking through a door (see John 20:19, 26). It was in His body that He experienced the return into heaven.

Like Him

Writing years after Christ's resurrection, the apostle John was not able to explain the constitution of the body with which Christians will be raised. He admitted, "Beloved, now we are children of God; and it has not yet been revealed what we shall be, but we know that when He is revealed, we shall be like Him, for we shall see Him as He is" (1 John 3:2).

Spiritual Body

Paul, exploring the same issue, wrote, "The body is sown in corruption, it is raised in incorruption. It is sown in dishonor, it is raised in glory. It is sown in weakness, it is raised in power. It is sown a natural body, it is raised a spiritual body" (1 Corinthians 15:42-44). A few writers have seized on this last expression as the basis for claiming that the resurrection will be spiritual only, not material. But Paul does not say "spirit-body"; he says "spiritual body," which implies a body controlled by spirit. In the same chapter (v. 49) he declares, "And as we have borne the image of the man of dust, we shall also bear the image of the heavenly Man."

Writing in Philippians 3:21 he stated that the change will be because of the Lord Jesus Christ, "who will transform our lowly body that it may be conformed to His glorious body, according to the working by which He is able even to subdue all things to Himself."

Recompense

Why a bodily resurrection? Two passages indicate that the body must be raised in order to receive the recompense for what has been done in the body: "For we must all appear before the judgment seat of Christ, that each one may receive the things done in the body, according to what he has done, whether good or bad" (2 Corinthians 5:10). "And I saw the dead, small and great, standing before God, and books were opened. And another book was opened, which is the Book of Life. And the dead were judged according to their works, by the things which were written in the books" (Revelation 20:12).

Applying the Truth
MY DAILY WALK WITH GOD

Draw a line connecting the idea with the scripture that supports it.

Resurrected bodies have some relationship with the bodies that died.	1 John 3:2
Christ's resurrected body appeared without walking into the room.	2 Corinthians 5:10
We don't know precisely how our resurrected body will appear.	John 20:19, 26
Bodies appear to be necessary for judgment to occur.	1 Corinthians 15:38

THE RESURRECTION: OUR HOPE

To the modern mind, the idea of the resurrection is inconceivable. It transcends nature. But to the God who out of nothing created nature and all that is in it, and to those who have faith in Him, it poses no great difficulty.

When a study is made of the sermons preached by the apostles, it becomes apparent that the great theme is always the resurrection of Christ. This experience authenticates Christ's message and establishes Him as He claimed to be, the Son of God. His victory over death seals the gospel of salvation.

Apostolic Preaching

The resurrection also becomes the Christian's greatest hope. "For the trumpet will sound, and the dead will be raised incorruptible, and we shall be changed. . . . Then shall be brought to pass the saying that is written: 'Death is swallowed up in victory'" (1 Corinthians 15:52, 54).

Greatest Hope

Paul concludes his resurrection treatise with this stirring injunction, with which we also conclude this study: "Therefore, my beloved brethren, be steadfast, immovable, always abounding in the work of the Lord, knowing that your labor is not in vain in the Lord" (v. 58).

LESSON REVIEW

The doctrine of the Resurrection is one of the most important and hope-filled teachings of Scripture.

Both testaments confirm the truth of the Resurrection. Although the Old Testament leaves many questions unanswered, the New Testament gives a fuller explanation of this vital doctrine. Still, however, mystery surrounds certain aspects of the belief.

When the apostles preached in the first decades after Christ's life, the great theme of their sermons—repeated over and over—was the bodily resurrection.

Both the just and unjust may anticipate resurrection, although their return in bodily form will occur at two distinct times. No precise information is revealed about the nature of the new body, but Christians are told that their resurrection body will be like Christ's.

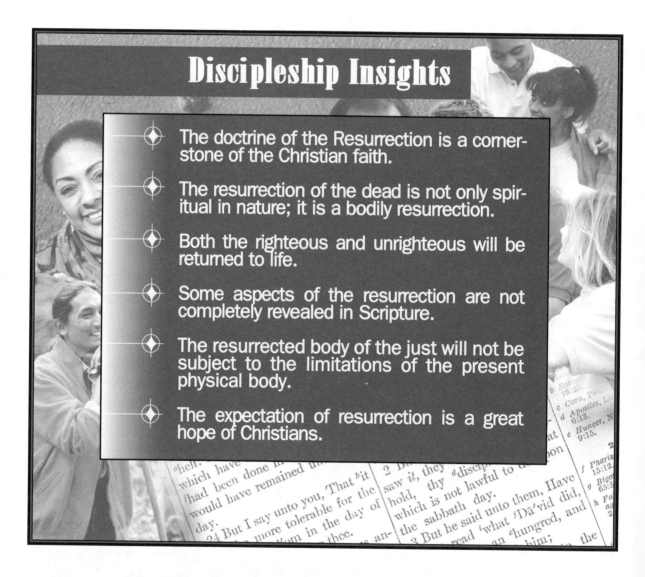

Discipleship Insights

- The doctrine of the Resurrection is a cornerstone of the Christian faith.

- The resurrection of the dead is not only spiritual in nature; it is a bodily resurrection.

- Both the righteous and unrighteous will be returned to life.

- Some aspects of the resurrection are not completely revealed in Scripture.

- The resurrected body of the just will not be subject to the limitations of the present physical body.

- The expectation of resurrection is a great hope of Christians.

Resources

Arrington, French L. *Christian Doctrine: A Pentecostal Perspective,* Vol. 3. Cleveland, TN: Pathway Press, 1994.

Bloesch, Donald G. *Essentials of Evangelical Theology.* Vol. 2, *Life, Ministry and Hope.* San Francisco: Harper and Row Publishers, 1979.

Fee, Gordon D. *The New International Commentary on the New Testament: The First Epistle to the Corinthians.* Grand Rapids: Wm. B. Eerdmans Publishing Co., 1987.

Ridderbos, Herman. *Paul: An Outline of His Theology.* Grand Rapids: Wm. B. Eerdmans Publishing Co., 1975.

NOTES:_____

_____

_____

_____

_____

_____

_____

_____

_____

_____

_____

_____

_____

_____

_____

_____

_____

_____

_____

_____